NEW NORCIA

New Norcia, 132 kilometres north of Perth, is unique in Australia; it is a town wholly owned by monks. Benedictine monks established a monastery here in 1846 and the town is now one of the most valuable elements of the National Estate.

The town now contains, besides the Monastery and its Abbey Church, some twenty houses, a hotel, a roadhouse, a trading post, old and new flour mills, the buildings that formerly housed a college for girls and one for boys, an 'orphanage' (effectively a boarding school for Aboriginal girls and one for Aboriginal boys), other school facilities now used for other purposes, and a collection of farm buildings and workshops.

The town is set within the bounds of the monastery farm, which covers about 8,000 hectares, more than a third of which is — and will remain — uncleared natural bushland.

From 1908 to 1982 the monks of New Norcia were also responsible for the mission to the Aborigines at Kalumburu in the far north of Western Australia.

New Norcia is named after Norcia, a city in the region of Perugia in Italy, the birthplace of St Benedict (480-543).

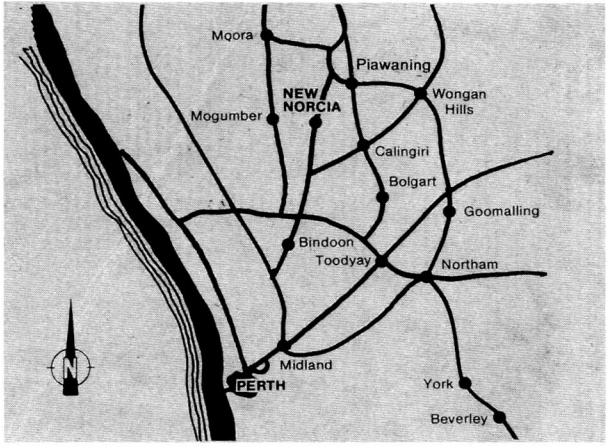

A TOWN LIKE NO OTHER

A TOWN
LIKE NO OTHER

The Living Tradition of New Norcia

EDITOR
DAVID HUTCHISON

ASSISTANT EDITORS
DOM CHRIS POWER OSB
AND WENDY PEARCE

FREMANTLE ARTS CENTRE PRESS

First published 1995 by
FREMANTLE ARTS CENTRE PRESS
193 South Terrace (PO Box 320), South Fremantle
Western Australia 6162.

Editor David Hutchison.
Designed by John Douglass.
Production Coordinator Linda Martin.

Typeset by Fremantle Arts Centre Press
and printed by PK Print, Western Australia.

National Library of Australia
Cataloguing-in-publication data

A Town like no other.

ISBN 1 86368 132 9.

1. Benedictines - Western Australia - New Norcia - History.
2. Benedictines - Missions - Western Australia - New
Norcia - History. I. Hutchison, D E (David
Eric), 1927- .

266.29412

Cover: *The Abbey Church* — a watercolour by David Gregson, 1993.

Page viii: *New Norcia from the east, 1860* — watercolour by an
itinerant artist.

Grateful acknowledgement to the
NATIONAL AUSTRALIA BANK
for financial assistance with the
production of this book.

NEW NORCIA A.D. 1860

All guests who present themselves are to be welcomed as Christ, for he himself will say: *I was a stranger and you welcomed me.* (Matt 25;35).

(The Rule of St Benedict in English, Chapter 53)

ACKNOWLEDGMENTS

The generous assistance and support of the following are gratefully acknowledged: the Staff of the Pictorial Collection of the Battye Library; the contributors and artists whose works have been included; and the scholars whose works have been quoted.

The Managing Editor of The Liturgical Press, St John's Abbey, Collegeville, Minnesota kindly gave permission to quote from their edition of *The Rule of St Benedict.*

The Western Australian History Foundation provided generous financial support for the preparation of this book.

The Editor thanks the Benedictine Community of New Norcia for friendship, support and hospitality.

Department for
theArts

Western Australia

The State of Western Australia has made an investment in this project through the Department for the Arts.

CONTENTS

INTRODUCTION

David Hutchison

My qualifications to be the editor of this book are my work as a museum historian, which first brought me in touch with the Benedictine Community some twenty years ago, and my membership of the Community's Archives, Research and Publications Committee.

That I do not share the faith of the Community might be a disqualification; it may be an advantage. My recent, closer involvement with the Community has enabled me to observe the Community's life more closely. I find echoes of this experience in a comment of Patrick Leigh-Fermor:

> ... in spite of these private limitations I was profoundly affected by the places I have described. I am not sure what these feelings amount to, but they are deeper than mere interest and curiosity, and more important than the pleasure an historian or an aesthete finds in ancient buildings and liturgy ... The kindness of the monks has something to do with this. But more important was the discovery of a capacity for solitude and (on however humble a level compared to that of most people who resort to monasteries) for the recollectedness and clarity of spirit that accompany the silent monastic life.[1]

This book is intended to help others to appreciate the richness and diversity of the life of this Benedictine Community. It is not, however, intended to be a detailed, critical history of the Benedictines in Western Australia. Not all facets of the Benedictine experience in Western Australia will be covered, or covered sufficiently, as the focus is on New Norcia. There is little about the Mission at Kalumburu; and the teaching of the Josephite Sisters and the Marist Brothers is only touched upon. The life of the Community is richly varied: not only devotion and discipline, but also music, architecture, literature and art; farming, blacksmithing, beekeeping, wine-making, the production of olive oil, milling, baking, printing, tailoring and shoemaking.

The Benedictine Order has a long history. It is not only

> the first of the great Western orders in time, but it held the field almost alone for several hundred years; and even when in the twelfth century it lost its monopoly and resigned its leadership in religious life, its influence continued to be supreme in the forms of worship used in the church.[2]

When I was invited to join the Archives, Research and Publications Committee, I felt that I should learn more about the Benedictines. Reading a translation of *The Rule of St Benedict*[3], I was surprised to find that it was not just an austere set of rules; it was also informed with the humanity of St Benedict.

St Benedict adopted an earlier rule, 'The Rule of the Master', but

> The difference between the two documents is immense. The Rule of the Master is diffuse, individual and indefinite in its liturgical detail, where Benedict's Rule is concise, universal and clear ... A comparison of the two documents leaves an unexpected impression on the reader's mind. Benedict, the most influential guide to the spiritual life in western history, appears as an uncomplicated and self-effacing man who was content to take nearly all his doctrine from the Rule of his predecessor. Yet with a few changes, omissions, and additions he changed the whole character of his source. He added strength where it was weak, tenderness where it was strong, and terseness and simplicity where it was diffuse and confusing. In so doing, he transformed an already remarkable document into one of the central statements of Christian living. He also produced the last great monument to the legislative genius of Rome.[4]

While Benedict required humility in the monks, he desired humanity in the Abbot. This humanity, which informs the austerity of his Rule, is that quality which I was surprised to find at first reading. Although the Order declined in the latter part of the Middle Ages, the Benedictines were

> ... for centuries the only guardians of literature, the classics, scholarship and the humanities in a world of which the confusion can best be compared to our own atomic era. For a long period, after the great epoch of Benedictine scholarship at Cluny, the Maurist Benedictine Abbey of St Germain-des-Pres was the most important residuary of learning and science in Europe.[5]

The heritage of New Norcia belongs in this long history of devotion, scholarship, art and music, which has a particular expression in the physical fabric of a town in the Western Australian wheatbelt.

Inevitably the book is limited by the bias — I do not use the word pejoratively — of a particular archive. For example, many of the early photographs used as illustrations were taken by one monk, Fr Santos Salvado, brother of Bishop Rosendo Salvado. Had there been many other photographers the images would have been more varied. What images might an Aboriginal photographer have offered us?

Although I have attempted to present the texts and images with minimal commentary, I am aware that the acts of selection and arrangement will have been affected by my own 'cultural baggage'. Tom Stannage shows how the representation of New Norcia in the history of Western Australia has evolved over 150 years in changing frames of analysis.

The story of New Norcia is a great story, with elements of tragedy as well as of achievement. For here was a meeting of a people with a culture at least 40,000 years old, with newcomers (invaders?) whose culture which, although it had roots equally as old, was the product of the two most recent millennia of European Christianity refined by the Rule of St Benedict.

The role of missionaries has been reassessed in recent times. In assessing the effects of the Benedictines on the Aborigines of New Norcia some allowance must be made for this reassessment, this change in a frame of analysis.

The founder of New Norcia appreciated the qualities of Aboriginal culture which, too often then — and now — has been dismissed as 'savage' or 'primitive'. His

Fr Santos Salvado in his room, c1870.
[*Courtesy of Battye Library 73332P*]

Fr Santos Salvado, Bishop Salvado's brother, was Chaplain of Queen Isabella II of Spain. In 1865, meeting his brother in Rome, he asked if he could be of use at New Norcia. His brother assured him that he would and suggested that he learn photography before coming. Fr Santos came to New Norcia in 1869 and took many of the earlier photographs included in this book. In 1879, aged 67, worried about eye troubles and fearing he might go blind, he returned to Spain.

temporary replacement as Superior, Fr Garrido, explicitly defended the moral values of that culture. However, the work of the Mission would inevitably displace that culture.

A former Abbot, Fr Bernard Rooney, shows that, within the Benedictine Community itself, there is a move to help the Aborigines to regain contact with their own culture. Perhaps paradox is inescapable for both missionary and editor.

WHERE WE ARE AND WHERE
WE'RE GOING

Fr Placid Spearritt OSB

Prior Administrator of New Norcia

The monks of New Norcia are under pressure. We are told that we must revive and develop connections with the Aboriginal community. We are also told that we must preserve the historical buildings, the art collection, the museum and library. We must preserve the archives and promote research and appropriate publication of their treasury of information on Aboriginal, colonial, local and church history; on the Colleges and the other religious communities who have worked in this town. We must protect and foster the ecological resources of the farm with its large tracts of uncleared bush supporting native plants and animals.

We must keep providing employment for the fifty-five or so people who work for us full-time or part-time. Most of them live locally and depend on off-farm employment to remain on their farming properties. If they can stay in the neighbourhood, we have a good chance of keeping the trading post open with its post office, and the roadhouse, and the hotel.

They tell us we must encourage more tourists and visitors, because without their spending the town cannot survive; and we must provide them with facilities, while at the same time controlling their numbers and their activities so that they do not destroy what they come to see, or spoil the distinctive monastic peacefulness of the town. We must bring more parties of school children to be educated by carefully devised programmes exploiting our diverse resources; and we must continue to house, in the former College buildings, the residential school groups of all sorts.

We must continue to provide the highly appreciated opportunities for adult groups and individuals to spend time in the monastery guesthouse, and in the other guest units that have sprung up across the road from the monastery as parts of other buildings become available.

These are some of the things people tell us we must do. I think that they are right; all of them.

The monastery can support all these projects, if it has its own house in order. For the house to be in order, our first priority has to be prayer, community and private prayer, the expression of our desire for union with God. Genuine love of God necessarily overflows into love of our neighbour, whom

Father Placid Spearritt, OSB, 1994.
[*Courtesy of West Australian Newspapers*]

The Chapel, 1993.

we take to be everybody in need. We must and we will do all that we can to provide for their needs, concentrating on the needs that can only or best be met by monks.

For that we need space for silence and reading, reverence for the traditions that we have received, for the Holy Scriptures and the sacred mysteries of the liturgy; we need intelligent, honest, and critical study of the ideas of the past and of the present, and openness to and deep respect for all the people with whom we come into contact.

And we need more monks. At present we are rather short of monks, and particularly young ones. Young people find it difficult to make a permanent commitment to monastic life, as they do these days to marriage. It is important for us not to panic in this situation, and certainly not to lower our standards of selection. The monastery can survive with a small number of monks if necessary; it is more likely to survive and flourish with a small number of good monks than with larger numbers of unstable characters. I like to hope that, as our community has had a multicultural history, its monks will reflect the multicultural composition of the church and world in which we live.

It is not quite true that the monastery can cope with all the needs I have mentioned. Good management of our resources in recent years has meant that we are able to provide for ourselves and for our religious work. But we cannot afford the outlay necessary for the conservation of the rest of the buildings apart from the monastery and the church, or for adequate provision for the art, museum, library and archive collections, or for the services and facilities that would normally be provided by a town or shire council.

I have talked with governments and many advisers about how to deal with these problems, and the answer seemed to be the establishment of a Trust Fund. Therefore, the New Norcia Heritage Trust was set up in 1995.

We have received a great heritage from the past. We want to administer it well and contribute further to it in the present, and pass it on to the future as a living organism. The monks' community is at the heart of it, but we have always wanted to share our inheritance with the people of Western Australia, and with students and visitors from further afield.

Some readers will be disappointed not to find here a grand vision for the future. You might have heard that the vision was the Aboriginal mission from 1846 to 1900; that it was the schools from 1908 to 1991; it was the mission in Kalumburu from 1908 to 1982; it was the Abbey Nullius from 1859 to 1982. That is what the romantic historians of New Norcia will tell you. I do not believe them.

The grand vision has always been a core community of monks who lived and prayed together and were open to the practical love of their neighbours *in whatever ways were most needed at the time*. This is my grand vision for the future too. A monastery that is defined in terms of some one definite work has got its priorities upside down. Besides, it is more exciting not to know too much in advance which way the Spirit of the Lord and the cries of the poor will direct us in the future.

THE AUTONOMY OF BENEDICTINE MONASTERIES

Benedictine communities differ widely among themselves, ranging from strictly enclosed monasteries to houses of monks active in schools, parishes and other apostolic works. Benedictines are called an 'order' only by comparison with later religious orders; each monastery is meant to be, and most are, fairly fiercely autonomous ... As monasteries differ from one another, so do monks. You will rarely if ever find two monks who agree on what a monk is, for instance, much less on what their monastery should be doing. So it needs to be stressed that the present writer is speaking for himself and for none of his confreres. Freedom of thought is a value almost as highly cherished among monks as it is among Anglicans. The astonishing thing is that monasteries survive for as long as they do — the average life span I have been told is about 250 years. That is perhaps evidence for some supra-human influence at work in the body monastic.[6]

Erecting the statue of St Benedict in the Cloister, c1933.
[Courtesy of Battye Library 72997P]

The statue was brought from Spain when the Diocese of Perth was under the administration of the Benedictines and, for many years, had the place of honour in the Cathedral in Perth which the Benedictines had built. When the new St Mary's Cathedral was built, extending the old structure, the statue was removed and eventually re-erected at New Norcia.

Corpus Christi Procession leaving the Abbey Church, 1930. Fr Alcade, Fr Ubach at the right of Fr Tubaru, Br Ildephonsus Martinez. *[Courtesy of Battye Library 78033P]*

Centenary celebrations, 1946. *[Courtesy of Battye Library 73814P]*

THE MONASTIC LIFE AT NEW NORCIA

St Benedict wrote his rule so that, 'by observing it in monasteries, we can show that we have some degree of virtue and the beginnings of monastic life.'[7] At the risk of oversimplification it may be said that

> the purpose of a Benedictine monastery is to develop and maintain a community of prayer — liturgical prayer, celebrated in common — nourished by personal study and piety and balanced by some kind of work which serves partly as recreation and partly to make the community self-supporting. In order to achieve this, or alternatively as a spin-off from having achieved it, monasteries through the ages have run farms, schools, hospitals and libraries or become centres of liturgical and historical scholarship and home bases from which a network of parishes or missionary stations have been staffed with clergy.[8]

The Community with visitors, 1965. The Apostolic Delegate, Archbishop Fustenberg, is in the centre of the front row. Abbot Gregory Gomez is on his right, and Bishop F X Thomas from Geraldton on his left. [*Courtesy of Battye Library 73108P*]

However,

> ... situations have often arisen in which there developed a tension between the essentially monastic or common life of prayer and the work of farming, teaching, or even preaching. As far back as the 'benign' Middle Ages, Chaucer had quoted with approval the old text 'A monk out of his cloister is like a fish out of water.'[9]

Fr Placid Spearritt expresses his vision of the Community being able to concentrate on the monastic life in future, and his concern that outwardly tending demands should not deflect the Community from its central purpose. We can see the emphasis on the community of prayer in the *Normal Horarium*, the programme for the monks of New Norcia:

MONDAY TO SATURDAY
0500 Rise
0515 Vigils (bell 0512)
   Private prayer, breakfast
0645 Lauds (bell 0642)
0730 Conventual Mass
   2nd sitting breakfast
   Free time
0900-1200 Work
1200 Angelus bell
1205 Angelus & lectio/prayer
   Sext
   Lunch
   Optional recreation
1330 Optional siesta
1435 None (bell 1430)
1445-1615 Work
1615 Optional afternoon tea
   Free time
1745 Quiet time / Lectio divina
1815 Optional rosary
1835 Vespers (bell 1832)
   Tea
   Free time
2018 Lectio/prayer & Compline (bell 2015) Great Silence until 0800

SUNDAY
0545 Rise
0600 Lauds (bell 0557)
   Private prayer, breakfast
0900 Conventual Mass
1130 Optional preprandium
1200 Angelus bell
1205 Angelus & lectio / prayer
   Sext
   Lunch
   Optional recreation
1330 Optional siesta
1615 Optional afternoon tea
1730 Vespers & Benediction
1815 Optional rosary
1830 Tea
1938 Compline (bell 1935)
   Optional TV; otherwise Great Silence until 0800

Variations on Saturdays
0830 Choir practice
2018 Vigils of Sunday (bell 2015)
   Great Silence until 0800

Left to right: Fr Stephen Lennon, Fr Justin Bruce, Fr John O'Shaunessy, Fr Theodore Hernandes, Br Placid Smith (Oblate), Fr Martin Lagninskie, c1957. [*Courtesy of Battye Library 72777P*]

St Benedict called his Rule 'a little rule for beginners.'

It contains directions for all aspects of monastic life, from establishing the abbot as superior, the arrangements of psalms for prayers, measures for the correction of faults, to details of clothing and the amount of food and drink ... St Benedict taught that if the monk seeks to answer the call of God — 'If you hear his voice today, do not harden your heart' — then he must put all else aside and follow the teaching of Christ in obedience ... Benedict was a keen observer of human nature and realised that people often fail (the abbot must 'distrust his own frailty'). He was concerned to help the weak, and consequently he enjoined the abbot 'so regulate and arrange all matters that souls may be saved and the brothers may go about their activities without justifiable grumbling.' Benedict looked to the heart; he sought a spirit of willingness ('First and foremost, there must be no word or sign of the evil of grumbling, no manifestation of it for any reason at all') and sincerity ('Never give a hollow greeting of peace'; 'Let us stand to sing the psalms in such a way that our minds are in harmony with our voices') ... He directed the abbot to 'arrange everything that the strong have something to yearn for and the weak nothing to run from.' It is a humane approach to personal relationships. But it is an approach based on the supernatural: 'that in all things God may be glorified.'[10]

St Benedict emphasised the need for the Abbot to lead by example; he must be aware

that the shepherd will bear the blame wherever the father of the household finds that the sheep yielded no profit. Still, if he has faithfully shepherded a restive and disobedient flock, always striving to cure their unhealthy ways, it will be otherwise: the shepherd will be acquitted at the Lord's judgement.[11]

The monks practise various trades and labours which are needed for the functioning of any community, be it religious or lay. Work is also a necessary discipline.

Idleness is the enemy of the soul. Therefore, the brothers

should have specified periods for manual labour as well as for prayerful reading.[12]

St Benedict also laid down the rules for the simple dress for the monks.

> The clothing distributed to the brothers should vary according to local conditions and climate, because more is needed in cold regions and less in warmer. This is left to the abbot's discretion. We believe that for each monk a cowl and a tunic will suffice in temperate regions; in winter a woollen cowl is necessary, in summer a thinner or worn one; also a scapular for work, and footwear — both sandals and shoes.
>
> Monks must not complain about the colour or coarseness of all these articles, but use what is available in the vicinity at a reasonable cost. However, the abbot ought to be concerned about the measurements of these garments that they not be too short but fitted to the wearers.[13]

The monastery produces much of its food, but its former vineyards have ceased production. Surplus products, such as olive oil, are sold. Although the flour mill was not functioning in the 1990s, the bakery returned to production in 1993. There are rules defining the way in which the monks will take turns to serve each other at meals. The meals are conducted in silence although, during them, one monk reads books on religious or secular subjects. St Benedict recognised that monks have individual needs for food and drink, and some will have weaknesses which they will be encouraged to master.

> For the daily meals, whether at noon or in mid afternoon, it is enough, we believe, to provide all tables with two kinds of cooked food because of individual weaknesses. In this way, the person who may not be able to eat one kind of food may partake of the other.[14]

> 'Everyone has his own gift from God, one this and another that' (*1 Cor 7:7*). It is, therefore, with some uneasiness that we specify the amount of food and drink for others. However, with due regard for the infirmities of the sick, we believe that a half bottle of wine a day is sufficient for each. But those to whom God gives the strength to abstain must know that they will earn their own reward.[15]

The monks are allowed recreation. Picnics (and, earlier, kangaroo shoots) were popular. Monks also take breaks away from the Monastery.

TITLES USED IN THE MONASTERY

Father David Barry, OSB.

Various titles have been used for monks at New Norcia; an explanation seems necessary. The title 'Father' is used for priests only, while 'Dom' may be used for all monks and novices. The title 'Brother' is no longer used at New Norcia; it was formerly used there for lay brothers.

In Spanish, the abbreviation 'Fr' is short for *Fray*, a contracted appellation of respect for all religious men, both monks and friars, whether priests or not. In French it is short for *Frere* (Brother), and is regularly used for monks, whether priests or not, and for abbots.

Although the title 'Brother' is not used in the monastery now, it is still the regular form of address for religious men who belong to a lay institution, eg. Christian Brothers and Marist Brothers.

'Dom' is short for *Dominus* — Lord, Master, or Mister. It is used for choir monks whether in priestly orders or not. Its use in New Norcia was more often than not reserved to choir monks and novices who were not yet priests; though it was used regularly for Salvado, even after he became a bishop and before he became an abbot. The distinction between choir monks and lay brothers was abolished at New Norcia in 1968. The title was re-introduced in 1979 as the ordinary title for non-priests and as an alternative to 'Father' for priests. It is seldom used in the USA except for Trappist abbots; in England it is usually reserved for monks in solemn vows.

Further research is needed to be accurate about the use of the term 'lay brother' at New Norcia. It appears that the Spanish words *converso* and *lego* had different denotations and, while the title given to both was 'Brother' (*Hermano*), *lego* was used to refer to a man who was admitted to the monastery and lived and worked with the community, but might only be received as a novice after some years; after the novitiate he would be eligible to make profession of vows. *Converso* would seem to have been used for a professed brother, which was certainly the case in the present century.

Members of the Community on a veranda of the Monastery, c1970.

[*Courtesy of Battye Library 72503P*]

A picnic at Hay Flat, September 1931.
[*Courtesy of Battye Library 74492P*]

Building the Carpenters' Shop, March 1926.
[*Courtesy of Battye Library 72827P*]

Three Brothers in the bush.
[*Courtesy of Battye Library 72523P*]

Novices with a lamb. [*Courtesy of Battye Library 72653P*]

Brother Vincent Burgos in the Tailor's Shop, 1960s.
[*Courtesy of Battye Library 72856P*]

Brother Vincent Burgos in the Butcher's Shop, c1966.
[*Courtesy of Battye Library 72852P*]

Brothers Peter Garbayo and Eugene Perez extracting honey, 1929.
[*Courtesy of Battye Library 72844P*]

Brothers Donato Arce and Paulino Gutierrez in the Bakery, 1928.
[*Courtesy of Battye Library 72847P*]

Brothers Donato Arce, Silvestry Lopez, and Placid Giminez in the Carpenter's Shop, 1929.
[*Courtesy of Battye Library 72848P*]

Brother Fulgentius Gonzales in the Book Binding Shop, 1929.
[*Courtesy of Battye Library 72849P*]

Brother Paulino Gutierrez in the Shoemaker's Workshop, 1929.
[Courtesy of Battye Library 73701P]

Brother Placid Giminez in the Power House, c1938.
[Courtesy of Battye Library 72841P]

Monks on a picnic, c1930s. [*Courtesy of Battye Library 74291P*]

Father Ubach and Brother Adalbertus Perez (in the driver's seat) with the first tractor at New Norcia, 1926. [*Courtesy of Battye Library 72843P*]

BISHOP ROSENDO SALVADO

Dom Joseph Serra and Dom Rosendo Salvado were co-founders of the Monastery of New Norcia. Serra, the senior monk in the earliest years, was appointed Administrator of Perth in 1849. After some frustrating delay, Salvado become the Superior of New Norcia and eventually the first Abbot. He remained Abbot until his death.

Salvado was born at Tuy, in Spain, on 1 March 1814 into a patrician family; he entered the Abbey of St Martin at Compostela in 1830. When the religious orders were suppressed in Spain in 1835, he took refuge at the Monastery of the Most Holy Trinity of Cava in Italy and was ordained priest in 1838. He arrived in Australia in 1846, was consecrated Bishop in 1849, and appointed Administrator Apostolic of New Norcia in 1859.

He demonstrated a rare courtesy and sympathy in his relations with the Aborigines and committed himself to his work in the new colony to the extent that he became a British citizen. His

Salvado in working clothes: serge trousers and blue denim shirt, 1850.

[Courtesy of Battye Library 66666P]

> respect and understanding for his Aboriginal friends shows in his writings ... which help to elucidate some important aspects of Aboriginal life.[16]

He was a polymath and an autodidact, mastering the details of astronomy, surveying, animal husbandry and whatever else he found necessary to develop the Mission. He explored the region for water and for pastures, mapping as he went, so making a substantial contribution to the knowledge of the region. On many arduous trips, and in the heavy labour of the farm, he displayed considerable resource, courage and physical endurance. He was not without his critics; they focussed on his occasional forays into colonial politics and his allegedly excessive acquisition of land for the Monastery.

He died in Rome in 1900, at the age of 86, at the Monastery of St Paul Outside the Walls. He had devoted 54 years of his life to New Norcia. His remains were later removed to his adopted country for burial at New Norcia.

REMEMBERING SALVADO

Mrs Fonseca, nee Miss Conway
(the first Postmistress at Berkshire Valley) [17]

Mr and Mrs James Clinch were entertaining Bishop Salvado in the drawing room of their beautiful home, Berkshire Valley. His Lordship was returning to New Norcia from Marah, in the late afternoon and the family were delighted when they realised he would rest there for the night ... When the family assembled in the drawing room with their distinguished guest, I, being not only the youngest, but almost a stranger, felt deeply impressed, as I listened to their conversations about their pioneering days; and when the Bishop related incidents of his last visit to Europe I realised in some measure the true characteristics that Mrs Clinch had spoken of, and I felt the influence of a great mind, a perfect spirituality, in his every sentence — so beautifully expressed — and his outstanding humility almost to that of a child! (Yet, ah! such a Princely bearing.) One felt drawn to kneel before him and listen on forever. He related of his visit to the Royal Palace in Spain ... Speaking of his return to Australia as 'coming home to my mission and children', he referred to their welcome on arrival at N. Norcia, and a pretty March composed for the occasion, entitled 26 — date of his return being 26 Sept. Thus speaking of music he turned to the piano. I suddenly remembered my lifelong childish desire to ask some great musician to express the meaning of the haunting little tune Pestal [?] in my 'Henry's Tutor'. His Lordship looked pleased, 'Yes, but first I will play it as I hear it being practised (*prestissimo*) when passing the houses in Perth'. He then played Pestal with an expression too deep for words, I could not restrain my tears as I listened.

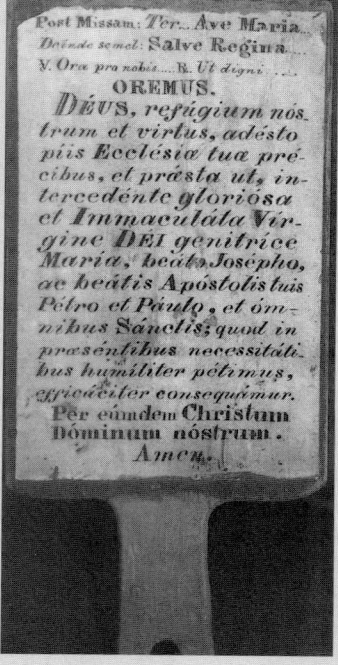

Salvado's sundial and compass.

Salvado's prayer chart.

Bishop Salvado with the family of Baron de Malda in Barcelona, 27 June 1885: Pilar,
Baroness, Baron, Concha, Ylino, Maria, Manuel, Dolores, Mercedes de Malda,
Salvado, Rosy Carcer.

THE GOOD SAMARITAN
ROBIN REDBREAST (DEMLARK)
A New Norcia Dreamtime Story

Trevor Walley

My great great-grandfather, Henry Indich, would accompany Bishop Salvado into the local bush to encourage Noongars to live at the New Norcia Mission. He died in 1896 and his grave and headstone, which were paid for by Salvado, can still be seen at New Norcia cemetery. My mother, at an early age, was put in the care of the Benedictine Sisters at New Norcia by her mother, and was kept there until her teens.

During my early life, I came close to being put in the New Norcia Mission. However, a Christian family, by the name of Corker, took us from the bush camp to live in their house. Some of my less fortunate cousins were living in poor conditions and had to be forced into the New Norcia Community. We often visited my relations there and talked with the Sisters.

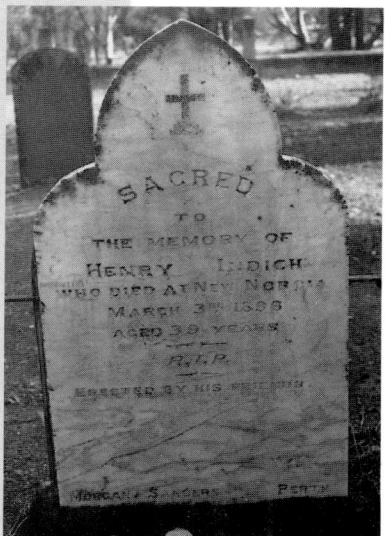

New Norcia Mission will always be seen as the saviour of, and home for, many Aboriginal people in those early periods when Aborigines were regarded, in the wider European community, as a cheap source of labour with no legal redress.

There are many stories known to my people from New Norcia. Noongar stories are like the ocean waves washing up on the beaches. Every wave changes the coastline and washes up something new. So with Noongar stories, which are told as new waves of people are washed up on the beaches. This is my favourite story:

It is said that the Robin Tribe heard of a person dying on a cross and bleeding from the wounds. The Robin Tribe went to help by rubbing their chests against the wounds to stop the bleeding. From that day onwards, the Robin (Tribe) Redbreast has a red breast to show the good deed and is considered almost a sacred bird.

Editor's Note: There is a similar legend about the robin redbreast in Europe. It is possible that the Noongar people heard this story from the monks and adopted or adapted it. It is also possible, and it would be interesting if this could be verified, that the Noongars invented the story themselves; an interesting example of a parallel invention of a legend in different cultures.

THE FOUNDATION OF NEW NORCIA

Salvado and Serra were fellow monks at Compostela and, later, at Cava and became friends. They decided to offer themselves for mission work, preferring to go together and in 1845 they were permitted to offer their services to the Congregation of Propaganda Fide.

Fr John Brady, who had been sent by the Archbishop of Sydney, in 1843, to take charge of a mission to be opened in Western Australia, went to Rome in 1845 to seek funds and missionaries. Brady and his party, including Serra and Salvado in a small party of Benedictines, arrived at Fremantle on 7 January 1846.

We are still in the middle of the bush, albeit within the city of Perth. One single house accommodates all the Missionaries together. We are all wedged in the same room, because this house only has the 6 rooms and twenty persons have to find a place.

Just this minute I learned that his Lordship is planning to dispatch us to the various posts of the mission one month or six months from now, but we do not yet know which place.[18]

One of the first annoyances was the displeasure the Bishop showed in having to supply us with what was needed for the Mission. Never would I have believed that a man could be so miserly about providing enough for other men to live on when they set out for a region where there is nothing but land and water and trees.[19]

After some delay, Brady — now Bishop of Perth — divided the mission into three districts. Serra, Salvado and two other Benedictines, Leandre Fonteinne, Denis Tootle[20], and an Irish catechist, John Gorman, were assigned to the Central Mission.

An Irish settler, John Scully of Bolgart, had advised Brady that several large tribes of Aborigines were camped in the valley of the Moore River, and he volunteered to act as a guide for the missionaries. The party left Perth on 16 February and rested for some days at the Scully homestead before undertaking the arduous trek in the bush. After struggling through rough going in very hot weather, they found that the spring that they sought, called Badji Badji by the Aborigines, was reduced to a muddy quagmire. They had to compete with their bullocks for the muddy water which did not quench their thirst, only 'plastered the inside of their mouths with an evil-tasting sand.'[22]

The weary and disillusioned party, still tortured by thirst, made camp for the night. At sunrise, Salvado, Fonteinne and one of Scully's men were guided by Aborigines to another place which was also dry. Fonteinne and the man refused to go on, but Salvado followed the Aborigine to another spring where there was water. Salvado returned and led his party to this place. The next morning was the first Sunday of Lent. Mass was celebrated before Scully's men left with the dray, leaving the party alone in the bush.

Aborigines watched them, but the monks made no approaches to them for a few days, until 2 March. The

Aborigines were invited to eat and work with the monks. When the monks believed that they had established good relations they asked if they could join the Aborigines in their nomadic life.

> With them we ate and drank and marched, and we volunteered for the tasks that they found most bothersome. Often we carried their children on our shoulders with their legs dangling down the front, and these took such a fancy to us that they preferred our company to that of their parents, which the latter took in good part.[23]

The monks began to learn the Aboriginal language and to study their customs. Although they did not admire some of their practices, others they did, including the care of the elderly and the sharing of food. However they began to suffer eye infections and other illnesses from their rough life in the bush. Salvado walked to Perth to seek help from Bishop Brady, but Brady offered none. Salvado made use of his musical talents, as pianist and singer, and, on 21 May 1846, staged a concert in the Perth Courthouse to raise funds. The concert was a success, musically, socially, and financially. It took some time for Salvado to purchase supplies and, during that time, Serra came to Perth with Dom Tootle whose health had broken down. While Salvado and Serra were in Perth, the Irishman Gorman was killed in a tragic accident.

> The only linen we brought was two shirts apiece, two pocket handkerchiefs, two pairs of stockings and the clothes we had on ... Besides our provisions we had two goats; I was leading them on a leash. We were heading across country through the bush. It was very dark. I failed to see a tree trunk and bumped into it so violently that I fell to the ground and the goats were so scared that they dragged me after them until the undergrowth stopped them.[21]

Salvado and Serra, now alone at the Mission, decided to leave 'this place of unhappy memories' and select a new site, which was more fertile. They built a second hut, ploughed a piece of land, and planted 'the kind of things we were likely to need.'[25] After some days of hard toil, Salvado made another arduous journey to Perth with the bullocks and wagon to collect the provisions that he had purchased. On the return journey he was lost temporarily and the wagon finally bogged, because of heavy rain, and had to be left for five months. The provisions had to be manhandled the rest of the way.

> Salvado and his small party had acted with due ceremony ... By actions showing ceremony, dignity and restraint, they had laid the basis for the rapprochement which was to follow with the indigenes of the Maura area.[24]

Although their crops were showing through by September, they were short of provisions by the end of October and their clothes were in tatters. They patched their trousers with kangaroo skins rejected by the Aborigines, and tied kangaroo gut around their waists to support them. They made boots out of wood and kangaroo skin. Salvado, however, claimed to be

WITH SWEAT AND BLOOD

Without losing heart, we went on with our agricultural labours; it was rather late in the season for sowing grain, but we cleared another piece of land and ploughed it. This was pretty awkward work for us, as we had no boots ... Father Serra drove the bullocks, while I managed the plough. To make the furrows deeper one had to push on the plough-share with one's feet, and these were badly cut by rocks and roots. So we ploughed that land not only with sweat but with blood.[27]

THE FIRST HARVEST

[By the beginning of September the monks had the great satisfaction] of seeing the green blades of wheat sprouting through the soil, and promising a good harvest. There was also the cheerful sight of 900 feet of vines, some fig- and lemon- trees; then rows of apricot-, peach-, and other fruit-trees (600 feet in all); there were many young olive-trees, and finally there were seed-beds of potatoes, carrots, radishes, tomatoes, parsnips, cucumbers etc.[28]

Father Augustine Cabane with William Bilyagoro, Salvado's 'first and greatest savage friend'. Salvado followed his 'cooee' and located Badji-Badji Pool in February 1846. Bilyagoro was baptised on 4 November 1846. He died on 5 November 1879.

[*Courtesy of Battye Library 73721P*]

An engraving prepared for Salvado's *Memoirs*: Father Salvado and Father Serra with Aborigines.
[Courtesy of Battye Library 77600P]

40

in better health than ever before, even if 'their external appearance was anything but impressive'.[26]

> As for fresh linen, I remember going once for three, and once for six months, without a change of shirt, and the one I had on would certainly not have survived the rain and my own sweat had it not been made of solid flannel.[29]

Despite their incredible labour and privations, the two monks continued to study the language and culture of the Noongar people, so that they 'could instruct them little by little in the Faith.' They also tended to the Aborigines' illnesses and wounds after spear fights. The women would frequently run to the monks and ask them to stop a fight.

> ... sometimes (we) managed to bring peace by our mere presence. At other times we found them so worked up and

Father Martinez baptising Michael Tacancut, whose wife and daughter Kathleen are sitting at his feet. His other daughters, Clara and Scholastica, are behind him. Calinga stands behind Father Martinez. The old man with the spear is Minga. Brother Fulgentius Dominguez is on his right. Tacancut's daughters were the first inmates of St Joseph's on 3 August 1861. c1867.

[Courtesy of Battye Library 73535P]

furious that, in spite of our efforts, they went on fighting savagely. Then we would take our crucifix and boldly step in between the contending parties; their spears came uncomfortably close, but we kept our presence of mind, pacified them with kindness and got them to hand over all their weapons to us.[30]

Salvado found that the Aborigines were secretive about their religious beliefs but, when he joined them as they gathered around a fire to cook and eat after a day's hunting, they narrated their legends and stories, and so he was able to learn some of their secrets.

He and Serra realised that they could not make real progress if they continued a nomadic existence, even though this had brought them in touch with the Aborigines. They went to Perth to discuss their plans with Brady, who saw that the establishment of a permanent mission was necessary, but he could offer no financial help. However, the Bishop received funds from Propaganda Fide and he gave Serra and Salvado a good share.

When they returned to the Mission, they found that a man sent by Brady to care for the Mission had allowed a mob of horses to break in. The fields lay in ruins; all their trees, vines and vegetables were uprooted and the furniture in their hut was broken. On top of that, a magistrate gave them notice to quit as the property had been leased to pastoralists. They did not despair but sought a new site. They selected

some land on the north bank of the river or stream that the English call 'Moore' and the natives 'Maura'. Here there was a natural rainwater basin, and both the soil and the position were better than in two previous localities ... We drew up plans for the twenty acres of land that the Government had authorised, and Father Serra went on foot to Perth and secured official deeds ... Meanwhile, beginning on 2 January 1847, I set to work building a hut on the new site and, although I was on my own, by the time Father Serra returned I had it all finished.[31]

Salvado's coat of arms — part of the murals in the Music Room.

Another twelve hectares of land above flood level were acquired as the site of the monastery and another 400 hecatres were granted them for grazing. During Salvado and Serra's visit to Perth at the end of 1846, many people had volunteered to help them.

'... THERE WAS ONLY THE WIND TO ANSWER MY VOICE'

A tragic accident in the bush

While Salvado and Serra were in Perth, Leandre Fonteinne and John Gorman were alone at the Mission. Fonteinne went hunting for game for food, but heavy rain forced him back to the hut.

> I found Mr Gorman sitting on the ground with his back against his mattress. He asked if I had spotted anything. 'Nothing,' I told him, 'the weather's too bad. The gun is wet, so I'm going to clean it up.' I moved over to a spot in the cabin where a towel hung; I take it up and am wiping off the gun. Meanwhile, Mr Gorman asks me what time it is. I turn aside to answer him. 'About twelve,' I say. And at that moment the gun goes off and the whole blast lodges in the head of my unfortunate friend, knocking off the skull top and scattering the brains ... My poor companion had uttered an 'Ah', which will resound for ever in my ears ... I let out cries for help in every direction, just as if I had been in an inhabited place. Alas, there was only the wind to answer my voice.[32]

Fonteinne fled to one of Scully's shepherds five kilometres away and, on the following day, went on to Scully at Toodyay.

> Since that blow my soul has not recovered. I have felt my vocation slip away from my bosom ... my mind has gone feeble and is no longer what it was, for although I have been reassured about God's judgement on me, inasmuch as my crime was involuntary, the refusal whereby I was not allowed to approach our kindly saviour has dealt my soul the final blow ...[33]

Fonteinne did not recover fully from this tragedy and he returned to Europe.

The monks began a second hut to house the volunteers and Salvado went to Perth in February 1847 to fetch them. The volunteers included Irish and French workers and 'an excellent Protestant bricklayer who had been inspired by God, the swayer of hearts'[34] to come to their aid.

The foundations of the monastery were laid on 1 March, the feast of Salvado's patron saint Rudesindus, just a year since they had celebrated their first mass in the bush. The walls were finished within fifty days, enclosing a space thirteen metres by five metres. When the roof was completed they installed a chapel and dedicated it to the Blessed Trinity, and named the place New Norcia 'in memory of the spot where our founder was born.'[35]

A BUSH FIRE
DECEMBER 1847

... one day, a poor native woman came running towards us pursued by her enraged husband brandishing a spear ... Neither we nor his friends could prevail against him. In order to prevent an awful crime, we took the unhappy woman to our cottage, the only safe place for her, and locked her inside. Finding himself thwarted in his evil intent, the maniac, gesticulating in anger and uttering terrible imprecations, left the Mission, whilst we continued our instruction ... on the following day we saw an inferno of flames devouring grass and trees alike and rapidly spreading towards our crop of corn, which we had partly stacked in sheaves. A high wind was blowing and within a short time a wide area of about a mile was burning furiously. Both we monks and the native ran to meet this danger to our crop and to the Mission. Following the native method, we used green branches to beat down the flames by sweeping back the parched grass, which was growing very thick and three feet high alongside the field where our crop lay ... We realised the help-

lessness. Unaided we could not prevent the complete destruction of the Mission ... we had recourse to God's Infinite Mercy through the motherly intercession of the special Patroness of our Mission ... We took the beautiful picture of Our Lady ... and placed it against the standing corn, which seemed about to catch fire at any moment. Then, with confident faith, we besought Her to look with maternal compassion upon our natives and ourselves. Merciful Heaven! No sooner was the sacred image of Mary placed in front of the raging fire than the wind blew in the opposite direction, carrying the flames away to where everything was already burnt black.[36]

Our Lady of Good Counsel.

THE SALVADO ERA

Once the monastery had been built, Salvado and Serra set about acquiring farm equipment, grain and stock. Salvado travelled many miles by foot in search of these. A track was cleared to Bindoon, over a distance of sixty kilometres, to link up with an existing track from that settlement to Perth. Importantly, for the future of the Mission, Salvado by this time

> had become a personality in the Colony. This could ensure credit when things were difficult and provisions and money were in short supply. It had become clear that upon him the raising of funds for New Norcia depended. Already, though Serra was Superior, New Norcia was being identified with Salvado.[37]

Within a year of his arrival in the Colony, Salvado had become a pastoralist as well as a missionary. He quickly learned the value of acquiring well-watered land and mastered

An engraving prepared for Salvado's *Memoirs*, showing the Mission, c1847.
[*Courtesy Battye Library 77606P*]

45

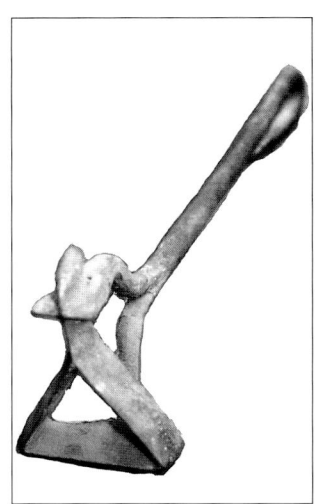

New Norcia's branding iron, using the symbol for the Holy Trinity.

the details of land regulations and the procedures for leases and land purchase. On all his exploration trips, accompanied by Aborigines, he surveyed and marked out potential leases. His skill as a surveyor and map-maker was acknowledged by colonial officials. By 1848 the Mission's leases totalled 7285 hectares; the mission had become a major pastoral enterprise. In time,

> The Monastery became famous throughout the colony for its up-to-date methods in farming and its successful experiments with new products. Its wool often fetched top prices in the London market, its horses were much sought after, its products won prizes at agricultural exhibitions, even overseas.[38]

Early in 1848, Serra had to go to Europe, leaving Salvado in sole charge of the Mission. In September news came that Serra had been appointed Bishop of the new settlement of Port Victoria (Darwin), news which distressed Salvado as it would lead to separation of the old friends.

In January of the following year, Salvado was ordered unexpectedly by Bishop Brady to go to Europe to deal with some affairs, to raise funds and to recruit missionaries. Salvado and Serra successfully recruited men for New Norcia. Salvado returned in August 1853 with three priests and thirty-seven lay brothers.

THE DIFFICULT YEARS

The Mission entered a very difficult period. Various circumstances would prevent Salvado from developing the New Norcia Mission for another eight years. As the Port Victoria settlement had not gone ahead, Serra was appointed Administrator of Perth in 1849. He evidently lost interest in New Norcia as a mission to the Aborigines and as the centre for the Benedictines in the colony. However, he used funds generated by the Mission to pay for a building programme in Perth and Fremantle.[39]

Salvado had been appointed, in Serra's stead, as Bishop of Port Victoria. He was able to visit New Norcia only with Serra's permission. This situation, and Salvado's struggle to have New Norcia made an independent diocese, must have caused tension and a sense of vulnerability among the monks.

Serra seemed to lose interest in the colony and became even more disputatious. He sailed for Europe in 1853, intending to resign as Administrator of Perth. Salvado was left in charge. Although he longed to return to New Norcia, which he visited frequently, he relished the wider scope for his abilities. He became even more popular in the colony as he set about repairing some of the damage which Serra's disputes had done within the Catholic Church and between the Church and society.

Serra returned in 1856. In the following year Salvado was permitted by Rome to return to New Norcia, although he remained under Serra's direction. He resumed his efforts to make the Mission independent of Perth and to improve the welfare of the Aborigines. He had a vision of a self-supporting mission village. He also set out to create a monastery as well as a mission. He founded a novitiate in 1859. In that year he

BISHOP SERRA

Serra was a cultivated intellectual, in contrast to the more pragmatic and entrepreneurial Salvado. Fonteinne thought that Serra was

> an excellent man, of truly holy piety. I believe he is far advanced in the ways of God. However, his character, formed in the Spanish mould, differs greatly from our French character. On the one hand it seems to be that his education did not inculcate in him those liberal principles which distinguish French education. [40]

A Catholic layman also wrote a character sketch of him:

> Dr Serra was a remarkably small man, with a remarkably large beard, in which he evidently took no small amount of satisfaction. He was also, to my mind, inordinately fond of jewellery, and of wearing his orders when opportunity offered. These are all pardonable weaknesses, but they displayed the character of the man. Personally he assumed all the dignity which he could command. Physically speaking he was a very small specimen of the genus homo, but mentally he could be called a giant. He was a perfect linguist and could speak French, German and Italian fluently. He was also esteemed an excellent classical scholar, while his knowledge of ancient and contemporary French history was simply profound. There was no European question with which he was not *au fait*, and he could, when he was so disposed, be most entertaining in giving accounts of European celebrities both in Church and State.[41]

Bishop Jose Serra, 1850s.
[*Courtesy of Battye Library 77996P*]

A LAY BROTHER COMMENTS

The diary of Manuel Beleda shows how uneasy life at New Norcia had been during the period of conflict between Serra and Salvado.

> ... the life we observed ... one can say could be like a very good Christian one but had nothing of the monastic.[42]

The diary also details the hard labour, and the training, including instruction in English, in British measurements, and in the tribal relationships of the Aborigines.[43]

> '... the Aborigines could generate fear and alienation. In Beleda's diary they hold a prominent place and a strong sense of caring and affection for them comes through as Beleda relates details of his pastoral work with them ... Yet there is also a sense of them, especially those Aborigines outside the mission, as "the other" ...'[44]

The strain was too much for some of the monks:

> Brother Rivera was bound as he wished to go out into the forest ... Brother Rivera escaped to the forest at 3 pm ... Brother Jose (and now Brother Esteban Tomas) begin to lose their reason.[45]

became Vicar Apostolic of New Norcia, but Abbot Casaretto, at Subiaco (Italy) was his Superior. The Benedictines who had been in the monastery built by Serra at Subiaco, near Perth, moved to New Norcia. An able monk, Father Garrido, came from Ceylon to become Prior, responsible for much of the internal organisation of the Monastery.

There had been moves to centralise control of Benedictine monasteries. Salvado believed that New Norcia was too far from Europe to be administered from there; the Mission's work was affected by conflicting demands from the Vatican, Propaganda Fide, and Casaretto. So he set out for Europe again in 1864, leaving Father Garrido in charge.

In Rome, Salvado was offered the Perth Bishopric, but pleaded to be allowed to follow his vocation with the Aborigines. Finally, in 1865, the Pope recognised that Salvado was the right man for New Norcia and, in March 1867, he decreed that New Norcia would become a Prefecture Apostolic and Abbey Nullius independent of Perth. Salvado would be Abbot for life and all Benedictine establishments in Western Australia were to come under his leadership. A Spanish lay brother expressed the relief of the community in his diary, 'the poor Mission was drowning in this jurisdiction'.[46] During this period, however, Salvado was frequently absent from New Norcia. Having been in Italy and England from 1864 to 1867, he returned to Spain in 1867. He had not been back long when he was called to Rome for the Vatican Council. In Spain and Rome it was obvious that he now had a high reputation in influential sections of the Church. He demonstrated that he was a vigorous and effective diplomat, negotiating with both civil and church authorities.

His visit to Spain was primarily to explore the possibility of establishing a missionary college to train monks for New Norcia. Through the support of Queen Isabella he came close to establishing his missionary college in a Royal establishment, the Escorial, but the political situation changed again in Spain.[47]

The Vatican Council ended hastily when Garibaldi's troops entered Rome and Salvado set out for home. During a visit to a

Benedictine monastery at Colombo, he had news that Father Garrido had died.

Salvado returned with some important recruits, including his brother, Father Santos, whom he appointed to succeed Father Garrido as Prior. He also brought forty-eight tonnes of baggage 'containing many precious ornaments and objects of art with which to enhance the rising Monastery of New Norcia'.[48] Salvado realised that the situation of the Aborigines in Western Australia had generally deteriorated; they were the victims of hostility or indifference. He knew that they needed the support of the law. In Governor Weld (1869–1875) he found a governor who was interested in Aboriginal affairs. Weld had been Minister of Native Affairs in New Zealand. Weld and Salvado became good friends and Weld looked on the latter as both his spiritual adviser and as his consultant on Aboriginal affairs. Weld achieved some progress, enacting various legislation. However — perhaps inevitably in the circumstances — these Acts made the Aborigines a 'protected people' and this may, in later administration of these Acts, have entrenched a paternal attitude.

The two decades of the 1870s and 1880s were devoted to the development of community life. Ornaments for the Monastery and books for the library were acquired. Under Brother Oltra music developed. Accommodation for the monks and cottages for the Aborigines were developed. The mission to the Aborigines and the farming activities appeared to be flourishing. With the building of a Post Office and a Court House, New Norcia was becoming a town.[49] Salvado was attacked during the 1880s because of the expansion of the land-holdings of his Monastery. He was accused of monopolising the best land and watering places. It was counterclaimed that the many wells sunk by the monks helped other settlers. Some criticism may have been because Salvado was more successful as a pastoralist than some other settlers. The size of the land-holdings was reduced as the native population declined.[50] Salvado returned to Spain in 1882 to try once again to establish a base for recruitment of monks for New Norcia. He also travelled in Italy, France and Belgium on monastery business; arranging for recruits, raising funds, and purchasing a wide range of goods and items. On 15 August 1899, he celebrated the golden jubilee of his consecration as Bishop. On 30 November he set out again for Rome, at the age of eighty-five. He had a busy year of negotiations, during which he selected his successor, Dom Fulgentius Torres. At Christmas 1900, he fell ill while staying in Rome. On 29 December, just before the end of the century during which he had achieved so much, he died. He was deeply mourned at New Norcia and by many in Western Australia who did not share his faith but who acknowledged his character and his achievements.

Father Garrido, 1870. [*Courtesy of Battye Library 77842P*]

ABORIGINES IN ROME

When Serra went to Europe in 1848 he took with him to Rome a seven-year-old Aboriginal boy, Benedict Upamera — the first Aboriginal boy baptised at New Norcia. Salvado intended that the boy be left there to complete his education 'in every branch of literature, science, and art'. He had a vision of an Aboriginal priesthood.

In the following year, Salvado took two more Aboriginal boys, Conaci and Dirimera, to Rome with him, at their own request. They were baptised John Baptist Dirimera and Francis Xavier Conaci by Bishop Brady. The boys were received by Pope Pius IX and Salvado also presented them to the King and Queen of the Two Sicilies. On 5 August 1850 they were installed at the Benedictine Monastery of Cava, where they chose to stay when Salvado returned to Western Australia.

The boys were admitted to the College of Nobles at Naples and were granted patents of Nobility by the King of Naples, news which the colonial newspaper, the *Inquirer*, was unable to report without a cynical comment that, on return, the boys would 'quickly sink their dignity and again resume their bush habits.'[51]

Tragically, they were not to be given a chance to show otherwise. Both fell seriously ill in 1853. Conaci died in Rome. The dying Dirimera returned to Western Australia with Bishop Serra. He was the only one, of six boys in all who were sent to Rome to lay the foundations of an Aboriginal priesthood, to return to the colony. He died soon after arrival.

Dirimera and Conaci (Konachi), two boys from New Norcia who accompanied Salvado to Rome in 1849 to become priests.
[*Courtesy of Battye Library 77930P*]

A POSTCARD TO REV FR BONIFACE

Toodyay 29/3/88
Dear Sir,
It is our intention to show a sample of our grubing [*sic*] machines at Victoria Plains races these machines are adapted for heavy clearing & are worked by hand you are requested to attend
Yours faithfully
Best & Kingston

A LETTER TO BISHOP SALVADO, 16 AUGUST 1889

The coffin sent by you is two [*sic*] small the lengtht [*sic*] is 5 feet 7 inc and two feet three acrost [*sic*] his Brest [*sic*] will you please send it as soon as possible as we are waiting.
Yours truly
C. Gee

AN ORDER FOR MOLESKIN TROUSERS

A memorandum to Salvado from Messrs G & E C Shenton, Perth, 10 October 1889:
6 doz pr Mole Trousers ordered for 1889 kindly state whether to be white or coloured or if you would like half white and half coloured or all white or coloured also 1 dozen burnished washing vessels are they to be enamelled inside to cost about 3/- each or painted to cost about 1/6 or 1/9.

A MEMORANDUM FROM THE MIDLAND RAILWAY COMPANY, 15 MARCH 1898

To Right Revd Father Damingues [sic]

I have on hand eight kegs of blasting powder and one case of carteredges [sic] also one Ball, these goods have been on hand since last Friday, I told the mailman to call and let you know so that you would be able to take it away as I was very buisy [sic] at the time and did not have time to wright [sic], I think he must have forgotten to call, I have your letter of 8th inst re the empty cask I will pay the Brother when he comes in, I think I owe you 13/-, 7/- for onions & 6/- for the cask ...

TWO PRESCRIPTIONS

A receipt for neuralgia

Perth June 15/89

My dear Lord Bishop

At last I am forwarding you the receipt for neuralgia, it is equal proportions of chloroform & sweet oil — to be well rubbed on the part affected, when rubbing on the part to be plunged into cold water & afterwards rubbed with a coarse towel. I suppose you will say 'There's plenty of <u>rubbing</u> about it'!

The chemist said that camphor dissolved in chloroform was also a very good remedy — of course I need scarcely tell you that both these remedies are <u>external</u> — although if the neuralgia arises from the teeth a small piece of wool dipped in the latter mixture & put into the tooth is good but care to be used in applying it.

I trust your Lordship has not had occasion to wish for this receipt & that it will be many a long day before you will require it ...

Believe me
yours very faithfully
E.W. Snook

A prescription for cough drops

Spirit of camphor .... one ounce
Aether, sulphuric .... one ounce
Chloroform .... two drachms
Sp. of wine up to .... four ounces

Pharmaceutical equipment on display in the New Norcia Museum.

A PURSE OF SOVEREIGNS FOR
FATHER COLL

Father Emelian Coll was the dispensing chemist at the Monastery. It is evident that he treated the illnesses of the people of the Victoria Plains as well:

Victoria Plains, Western Australia
20 May 1892

To the Reverend E. Coll
Order of St Benedict
New Norcia Mission

Reverend and Dear Sir,

Under a grateful sense of the many kindnesses received from you in the time of sickness during many years that this District has been without a Medical Officer we request that you will be pleased to accept the accompanying purse of sovereigns and that this small token may be put to some use that may remind you of the many grateful friends that you have endeared yourself to by your ever ready and willing Christian help in giving relief to those who have sought your medical aid and skilful treatment on so many occasions.

We trust that you may be spared for many years in health and happiness and now beg to remain

Your sincere and grateful friends,

H B Lefroy	W Elder	C. Greenwood
Rose A Lefroy	W Hogan	J. Shannon
Mary Lefroy	A Bracken	Peter Dix
Langlois Lefroy	Mrs B Joyce	John Dix
William Campbell	H Joyce	Misses Clinch
J McGibbon	Mrs Donald	(West End)
Ben Martin	McPherson	W P Boxhall
Kate Joyce	Brooke Evans	M Lannigan
Amelia Joyce	J & J Clune	A Poynter
Thomas Knight	Thomas Fitzgerald	Edmund King
George Taylor	John Brown, sen.	Owen Lavin
Tom Joyce	James Butler	W Padbury
Stephen Sheridan	Andrew Lannigan	C K Davidson
John Elder	Richard Lannigan	Mary Dix
W D'Arcy	Mrs Hardey	Mrs Halligan
T Betts	Mrs Evans	H Powell
Aleck Betts	C. Gee	Mrs Powell
James Gladwell	W. Pead	James Hunt
James Thorley	R. Broad	T Anderson
James Gallagher	Lizzie Regan	

Marah Victoria Plains
Western Australia
16 June 1892

To H B Lefroy Esq JP
Dear Sir,

I am quite at a loss how to express my most sincere thanks to you for the great trouble taken in coming to Marah for the sole purpose of handing over to me personally a purse containing thirty sovereigns, with an Address signed by sixty of this District's Residents. The Address gives vent to most grateful sentiments towards my person as emanating from those who sought my medical treatment during the many years the District was without a Medical Officer.

I hope that those who signed the Address, as well as those who did not sign it, did not labour under the impression that such course taken was required to remind me of the gratefulness for what I have done to relieve their ailments; they may be assured I have not forgotten the many tokens of kindness manifested to me in many ways and on many occasions, though the poor sufferers could, I am sure, but plainly see, to their detriment, how so very limited was the medical knowledge I possessed.

Now, Dear Sir, be pleased to convey my most sincere sentiments of gratitude to all who so kindly signed the address above alluded to whilst wishing health and prosperity to them all.

I remain
Dear Sir
Yours most thankfully

E Coll OSB

Father Emelian Coll with pupils, 1867.
[Courtesy of Battye Library 73474P]

55

LANDSCAPES
HAVE THEIR VOICES ...

Elizabeth Jolley

In 1977 Father E J Stormon, translator and editor of Dom Salvado's *Memoirs*, wrote to me.

> It was good of you to think of me when you were visiting New Norcia. The card [you sent] evoked some happy memories, since, during my time in the West, I was often there: I liked the peace and the friendship of the community, and the countryside, through which I took long walks, was of the kind that spoke to me, probably because I spent an impressionable part of my boyhood in similar country about fifty miles, as the crow flies, to the south-west. Landscapes have their voices, I find, if one is responsive and attuned, though what they say doesn't go into words ...

I saw the landscape of New Norcia unexpectedly, coming upon it, without previous knowledge, on my way to another place. The surprise of the idyllic and tranquil scene remained with me, as I saw it then, throughout subsequent years — even after further visits. This first view was before the publication (and my consequent reading) of Father Stormon's translation of *The Salvado Memoirs*. On that occasion I did, without realising it, what foreigners to this country are said to have done with landscape, trees, flowers and birds, from the time when the first explorers set foot in Australia; I put an image of the once familiar countryside in England over the face of the land where New Norcia is. I did not do this in a critical or detailed way but rather in an impressionistic way. I saw the curves of the land before me as if gently folded and green to the very doors of the buildings as in Wordsworth's poem:

> These plots of cottage-ground, these orchard-tufts,
> Which at this season, with their unripe fruits,
> Are clad in one green hue, and lose themselves
> Among the woods and copses, nor disturb
> The wild green landscape. Once again I see

These hedgerows, hardly hedgerows, little lines
Of sportive wood run wild: these pastoral farms,
Green to the very door, and wreaths of smoke
Sent up, in silence, from among the trees.
With some uncertain notice, as might seem
Of vagrant dwellers in the houseless woods,
Or of some Hermit's cave, where by his fire
The Hermit sits alone.

These lines, from 'Lines, composed a few miles above Tintern Abbey on revisiting the Banks of the Wye', seem to hold the essence of New Norcia, the cultivation in a landscape cleared from the surrounding 'sportive wood run wild', 'the houseless woods', that is the Bush. And the idea of 'some Hermit's cave' and 'The Hermit sits alone', the silence of the life in the monastery, and the reference to plots and orchards all make this picture which was, to me, easy to transplant from the country of origin to the new country.

I remember on another visit, still passing through, leaving the car to walk beside the buildings that line the road. These strong, solid, ornamental buildings, which were then boarding schools for boys and girls, were painted with thick, richly coloured paint. It was easy to imagine my own remembered weeping in some secluded corner of my own boarding school. The bitterness and wastefulness of homesickness is never forgotten and the school buildings at New Norcia, in spite of all the goodness and devotion to well-being within those walls, will have well-remembered spots where real isolation and homesickness have been experienced. On that occasion I walked all about New Norcia in the air which was clean and dry and light, air which makes a person immediately feel better. The cape lilac trees on either side of the path to the entrance to the pro-cathedral were in sweet scented flower, adding to the well-being of the traveller.

Perhaps I can suggest that, instead of passing through, the traveller spends some time there to experience the peace and the kindness, the tranquillity of the landscape and the fresh air. I suggest, too, that the traveller reads *The Salvado Memoirs* to experience the real truth of the good *intention* which was accompanied by stout hearts.

Warm coloured brick walls are a feature of New Norcia, 1993.

St Gertrude's College, 1993.

THE ABORIGINES AT NEW NORCIA

A full assessment of the impact of the Benedictines on the Noongar people has yet to be written. Salvado, by force of personality and a genuine empathy for the people he called 'The Australians', gained their trust. But his aim was to convert them to Christianity, however much he respected many aspects of their culture. He also sought to train them for 'useful employment'. He did not share the contemporary view of most of the colonists, that the Aborigines would die out, giving way to a 'superior civilisation'. He founded

> The largest and most adventurous mission enterprise in the south-western area ... The monks sought to teach the Aborigines of the area to become peasant farmers, as well as to convert them to Catholicism, and they placed a heavy emphasis on learning practical skills that would equip Aborigines for life in the settler society.[52]

However, Salvado had a wider and deeper interest in Noongar culture. When he was surveying the new track to Bindoon in 1847 he came across a large number of Aborigines who were strangers to him. Salvado was introduced to them by one of his Aboriginal companions and a solemn ceremony of greeting, involving mutual embracing and exchange of weapons and products of the hunt, ensued.

Brother Pablo Clos nursing a boy, Pat. The Aboriginal man wearing an emu feather sash is Chiuk; the other is Biug-an.
[Courtesy of Battye Library 73545P]

> Then in a solemn tone the eldest of the strangers addressed our oldest member ... 'Here is my fire, now it is yours too. I stay here; you come and go, then you come back to go away and come again, and then you stay; now we are great friends.' I ... was surprised to see demonstrations of courtesy that suggested civilised man rather than the savage.[53]

This passage reveals not only Salvado's ability as an observer and recorder, but also his instinctive respect for the Noongars and their customs. In the ceremony which he reported, Salvado had recognised the Aboriginal concept of ownership of land, and that he was, in effect,

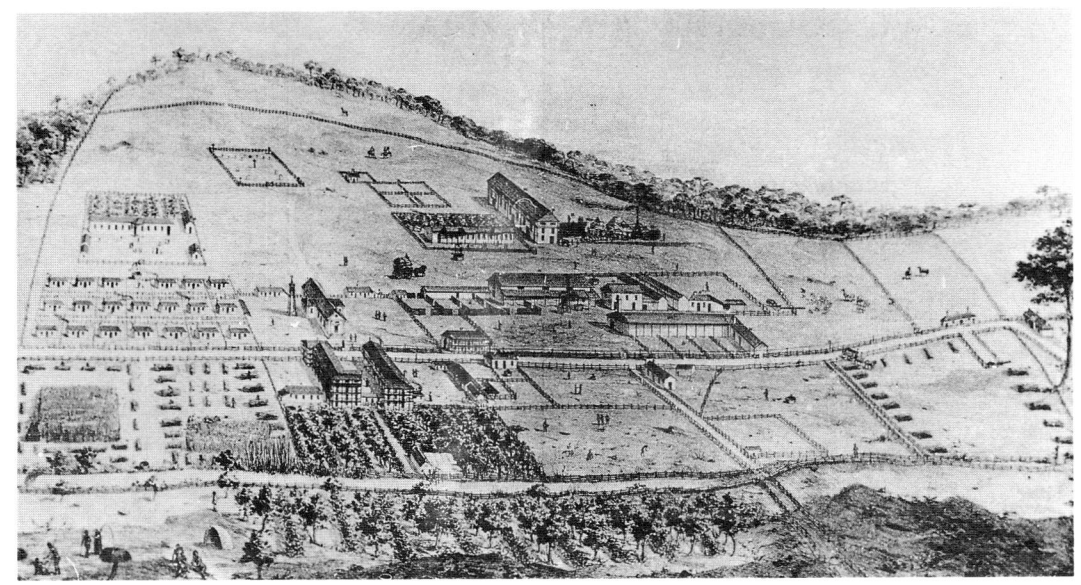

A sketch of New Norcia c1880, showing the location of the Aboriginal cottages.
[*Courtesy of Battye Library 73614P*]

View of the Mission during Feast Day celebrations, 1882.
[*Courtesy of Battye Library 73622P*]

being granted a 'temporary easement', with right of passage.[54]

> Salvado appreciated the nuances of Aboriginal law and lore. He responded with the sensitivity of an artist and mystic to the dignity and charisma of Aboriginal elders and the intricacies of Aboriginal ceremony and society. At the same time he recorded with exemplary scientific precision the details of diet and demography, land and society.[55]

The attempt to educate the Aborigines began on 8 December 1847, the feast of the Immaculate Conception.

> ... the College of New Norcia was opened for their sons. As the fruits of heaven's blessing three boys were admitted there and then. These had left their families of their own free will, and with their consent stayed with us henceforth ... [56]

A rough hut was erected, dignified with the title of Orphanage and School, named St Mary's. Some of the Aborigines, including those who earlier would not hand over their children, became offended because their boys had not been taken into the Mission.[57] Girls were sent to Perth at first for education by nuns. St Joseph's Orphanage for girls was established later. The work with the children was suspended during Salvado's absence overseas from 1849 to 1853. When he returned as Superior in 1859

> he infused new life into the half-dead body of the Mission in general and the Boys' orphanage in particular.[58]

A DEFENCE OF THE MORAL VALUES OF NOONGAR CULTURE

In 1867, Father Garrido was acting as Prior in Salvado's absence. In his annual report to the Colonial Secretary he strongly defended the moral values of Noongar culture.

> ... it is difficult to believe all that is asserted about their intellectual inferiority by travellers and other writers. They are, it is true, quite ignorant of the simplest arts of civilised life; but they have their own standards of right and wrong, which no argument of the white man can change. Good action and good morals they acknowledge, and praise as 'kuoba', right: whatever is bad they regard and express as 'winda', wicked. If occasionally the wilder aboriginals find a difficulty in defining the difference between killing a sheep and killing a kangaroo, both of which feed on grass, and roam at large in the bush, it should, before condemning them, be settled which of the two shows the greatest dullness of moral perception — the unauthorised occupiers of their woods, who themselves kill as many kangaroos as they can, or the original owners of that land who take such things as they find upon it, looking upon them as their legitimate means of subsistence.[60]

Aborigines began to join in the monks' work: tilling the soil, planting crops, road and bridge construction. Portions of seeded land were allotted to Aborigines who had helped.

> It was wonderful to see the care which each one took over his own section ... And these the same natives who had poked fun at us when we ploughed the land, and thought we were quite mad when we put in seed.[59]

The first St Joseph's Orphanage.
[*Courtesy of Battye Library 74609P*]

The second St Mary's Orphanage.
[*Courtesy of Battye Library 74245P*]

Encouraged by their response, Salvado tried the incentive of paying them, but they tended to lose or give away the money. Salvado got them to understand that, if they saved the money, they might buy stock. He encouraged them to hand the money to him for safekeeping. He had a compartmented box made, one compartment for each man, to hold these savings. Some asked Salvado to build houses for them.

In 1860, a larger though still unpretentious building of slab and clay replaced the original St Mary's and a brick cottage was added a few years later. The earlier buildings were demolished in 1924 when the new St Mary's was completed.

In 1860 a measles epidemic wreaked havoc in the local population and, later, measles and influenza almost obliterated the traditional landowners of the district. Salvado then began to seek children from beyond the Victoria Plains.[61] Salvado regretted that the Masters and Servants Act (1874) did not require Aboriginal children to remain at school and urged that the Education Act (1871) should be changed to require Aboriginal, as well as white children, to attend school. His lobbying appears to have been successful as the Industrial Schools Act (1874) was directed to the education of Aborigines and gave the principal of New Norcia, and of similar institutions, the same authority over the child as the child's father. The number of children at New Norcia increased rapidly after 1874. By 1875, the number of Aborigines at the Mission reached 180; the number declined to 122 in 1890, but rose to 134 by 1892.

In the 1890s the Forrest Government reduced subsidies to the missions; many Aboriginal families were forced to leave New Norcia to find employment elsewhere. The landholdings of the Mission were reduced from nearly 400,000 ha in 1900 to just over 41,000 ha in 1909.

Until about the turn of the century the boys were kept at the institution until they married. There were, therefore, always boys at the Orphanage who were above school age. They lodged at the Orphanage but worked under various lay Brothers during the day. However, there were, by then, few lay Brothers and they were ageing. The upper age limit at St Mary's had to be reduced to make room for younger boys. Most of those now entering were grandchildren of Aborigines born and reared at the Mission.[62]

When Abbot Torres followed Salvado, the policies of the Mission changed. Torres looked further afield for Aboriginal mission work, establishing the mission at Kalumburu. He also built the two colleges for non-Aboriginal children. Institutional care for Aborigines continued, but no longer had priority.[63]

By 1904

> The orphanage aspect of the mission's work was receiving an increasing emphasis, as a departure from the original idea of a village of family groups tilling the fields in the precincts of the monastery, and as a reflection of the growing number of children of mixed descent born of unions which did not persist ... [64]

In that year, a Royal Commissioner inquiring into the condition of the Aborigines visited New Norcia and found it in a flourishing condition, doing excellent work, and worthy of government support.[65] On 28 December, the Commissioner questioned Father Edmund McCormick at the Mission; his replies provide a 'snapshot' of the Mission soon after Salvado's death and early in the reign of Torres.[66] Some of the replies are summarised here:

The policy of civilising and Christianising the Aborigines was still kept in view. There were two missions connected with New Norcia, at Marah and Wyening. There were about six to nine Aborigines at both outstations. They were provided with cottages similar to those at New Norcia. The Aboriginal children at the Mission attended school for two hours each day; their curriculum included the three Rs, a little geography and the Catechism.

Girls were taken into the Convent at three or four years of age, or even younger, and remained there until they married. When 'old enough' they did a little work; gathering olives and helping to make the oil, and a considerable amount of mending for the community. They had to do their own cooking and washing.

The boys worked in the gardens or the fields; they remained at school until thirteen or fourteen. From the age of seventeen or eighteen they received wages; until then they were provided with board, clothing and a little pocket money. Wages for Aboriginal boys and men ranged from £1 to £3 per month. (It should be remembered that Aboriginal workers employed on stations were usually paid little, if anything, other than keep until much later.)

When an Aboriginal couple married they were married according to the rites of the Church and the law of the land. Each couple was provided with a furnished cottage free of charge, but had to buy their own provisions other than some fruit and vegetables from the Mission garden. Goods were sold to them by the Mission at cost. There were twenty-six brick cottages for natives at the Mission; they paid only a nominal rent of one shilling per annum. Some families were fairly well

Two Noongar youths being baptised by Father Martinez. [*Courtesy of Battye Library 73522P*]

Matthew Colcop, a horse-breaker from Gingin (seen when younger in photograph to the left), c1869.
[*Courtesy of Battye Library 73695P*]

Br Romualdo Sala with Colcop and two girls, the taller Warichiau, the other is Bug-nan (Bouyacan), c1860.
[*Courtesy of Battye Library 73684P*]

Mrs Judith Butler (school-mistress) with Frances Mingal, Eliza, Elena Tainan, and Cecilia Yaki, 1867. [*Courtesy Battye Library 73694P*]

off and applied for forty to eighty hectares of land; others preferred to 'make back to the land'.

There were about two hundred Aborigines and half-castes at the Mission: thirty-nine boys and twelve girls at school. Some of the families at the Mission were now in their third generation. During the previous twelve months only one Aborigine had left the Mission of his own free will, and he returned. Three had been sent away. Only one case of drunkenness had occurred in recent years; he knew of no cases of venereal diseases. He objected to a report by Mr Prinsep on half-castes at the Mission; he had alleged that their behaviour was not as good as full bloods. The report seemed to be based on Prinsep's experience with one half-caste who had left the Mission.

It was evident also that the Mission had not given up its vision of an Aboriginal priesthood. Father McCormick stated that

... it is the Abbot's intention to erect a new monastery here in which he will be able to provide for 100 Australian brethren. It is the intention, if possible, to establish a separate community in Australia, that is a community independent of the House at home, and that they should be natives of the country.[67]

At about this time the Mission restricted access of Aboriginal parents to their children, and began to deny it. In 1907, Aborigines, led by Emmanuel Jackamarra, George Shaw and Lucas Moody, stormed the Mission orphanage to free their children. They were not successful and the three men were arrested and jailed for disorderly conduct and for damaging Mission property.[68]

By 1946, the one hundredth year of the institution, more than seven hundred boys had passed through St Mary's. St Mary's and St Joseph's were retained as Aboriginal institutions until the 1960s. Government policy then changed and discouraged institutionalisation of Aboriginal children and separation from their parents. Some Aboriginal children remained at New Norcia as pupils of the new Colleges.[69]

... the Benedictine Mission can probably claim to have been the most humane, consistent and successful attempt at civilising and Christianising the Australian Aborigines undertaken anywhere in the nineteenth century. Yet ... it is also necessary to say that it failed. Fifty years of devoted and imaginative work by Bishop Salvado and his monks did not succeed in converting the Aborigines into the Christian, small farmer families he seems to have envisaged. By the time of his death in 1900, in fact, there were very few Aborigines left in the area around New Norcia ...[70]

Economic factors may have been involved in this failure as well as changes in Mission and Government policies. Premier Forrest's vision of a sturdy 'yeomanry' on relatively small holdings in the wheatbelt proved illusory. As late as the 1930s, Premier Mitchell's similar vision of establishing small farms in the cleared forests of the south-west failed abysmally. Neither premiers understood the limitations of climate and soil militating against smallholdings in Western Australia.

William Monap and his wife Scholastica Nangulan. Their wedding was conducted with great pomp on 25 November 1866.

[Courtesy of Battye Library 73549P]

Eliza Tainan, c1908. She had been at the Mission for thirty-six years and was, by then, widowed. She cooked at St Joseph's and was skilled at needlework.

[Courtesy of Battye Library 73548P]

Bob Nogolgot with his wife Joanna (Pagneran) and children. Both
belonged to the Bindoon tribe, and were of great assistance to
Bishop Salvado in the early days of New Norcia, 1860s.
[*Courtesy of Battye Library 73556P*]

Aboriginal housing at New Norcia, c1950.
[*Courtesy of Battye Library 74420P*]

Harry Wag-lio and his wife outside their shingle-roofed cottage, c1875.
[*Courtesy of Battye Library 73688P*]

Dicky Tondoroik and his wife Mary Louisa
Gnarnet, 1870. [*Courtesy of Battye Library 73693P*]

Aboriginal girls at their first Communion, 1930s.
[*Courtesy of Battye Library 74266P*]

Two St Mary's boys dressed as monks for a fancy dress party, c1946.
[*Courtesy of Battye Library 73018P*]

Alfred Cuimara (Quimera) and his wife Sarah Ilbichau celebrating their golden wedding with forty-eight of their children, grandchildren, and great-grandchildren, 1935.
[*Courtesy of Battye Library 72700P*]

THE MISSION:
A FIRST-HAND EXPERIENCE

Ben Drayton

The family names Taylor and Quimera have been associated with New Norcia from before the 1870s. Today descendants of Alfred Quimera still work the mission property. My mother, Mary Consuelo Taylor, was the daughter of Melchior and Angelina Taylor and spent most of her life at New Norcia. Her grandfather was an Englishman, William Smith, a convict, possibly brought to the Mission to assist with the building.

My father, Robert Joseph Drayton, was brought to New Norcia as a baby, from the Geraldton–Carnarvon region. Both my mother and father worked for the community in various jobs and later became Oblates of St Benedict. They were buried with this distinction in New Norcia.

I can comment only on the period from 1954 to 1968, my own schooling and early working life. We were educated by the Benedictine sisters and two areas were emphasised: religion and discipline. A typical day for the younger boys began at 6.00–6.30 a.m., serving mass for priests at the church. Breakfast followed: no more than a plate of porridge, or sheep's head broth, or 'weeties'. After breakfast we were rostered for chores, including washing dishes and sweeping floors. School was about one kilometre away and we had to walk there, in bare feet, in weather which was sometimes hard to cope with.

There were four schools in the town; two for Aboriginal students and two for European students. Both communities were segregated, rarely interacting except at sport. The sisters took us for all lessons which included reading, writing, arithmetic, religion, art and geography; a large part being taken up with learning hymns and singing mass in Latin. Classes were co-educational. Sometimes it was hard to understand the Spanish teachers. I am sure this caused many students to be punished for not understanding directions.

Schooling lasted to Year Seven. Older boys then left the orphanage or were employed on

Patrick Walley, Gabby Willaway, Mick Indich, Victor Worrell, Les Williams, Fred Spratt, 1966.
[Courtesy of Battye Library 72962P]

St Mary's Orphanage, 1950s. [*Courtesy of Battye Library 74117P*]

Father Eladio Ros and boys picking olives, 1935.
[*Courtesy of Battye Library 74559P*]

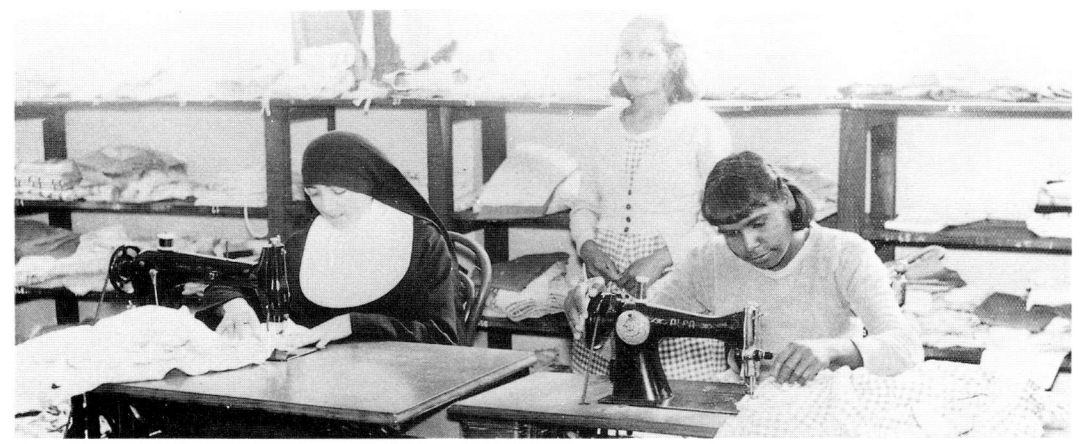

Sister Carmen Ruiz, Angelina Moody and Margaret Newell. [*Courtesy of Battye Library 74250P*]

A school room c 1960. [*Courtesy of Battye Library 74236P*]

A procession from the Abbey Church, 1860s. [*Courtesy of Battye Library 73621P*]

the mission property. The girls' experience was similar, but theirs was hard in comparison to the boys'. Older girls were encouraged to stay on longer because of the work: cooking, washing, ironing, sewing and other chores for the monks and for the boys' and girls' schools. There was also olive and orange picking, and cleaning the church.

Sport was also a feature: football, cricket, netball, hockey and athletics. Many times the school excelled in sporting events against other schools. On weekends and feast days the boys especially were allowed to go on bush walks. The girls had their own outings. Mass was essential every day in the boys' chapel, and on feast days and Sundays in the church.

I was lucky to be invited to continue secondary studies at St Ildephonsus' College, which was controlled by the Marist Brothers. I was chosen, with three other boys, because my handwriting was neat. However, I was not prepared properly in most subjects and was like a fish out of water. At the end of second term I excelled in Latin and religion, with marks over ninety per cent, but failed in other subjects. Was this due to teachers at primary level?

It was a very difficult time for everyone. Boys and girls were brought to the orphanages from all over the State. In many instances they were brought in at a very early age and spent most of their childhood at the orphanages, losing their identity and family background. Aboriginal language and culture were banned, mainly because the care-givers did not understand what the boys were saying.

Those who could cope with the system conformed. Those who were constantly on the wrong side of the priests and nuns found it a hell on earth. At times I felt like running to my parents, who were one kilometre away, but I was not allowed to. It certainly was not a bed of roses. What did Bishop Salvado set out to do in the first instance? Was it to convert the people, was it to educate the people, or was it humanity in response to the displacement by white farmers? Maybe it was all three. However, I believe that the priests who followed Salvado have not upheld his beliefs and works. There appears to have been a continual shift in their goals.

The friendships built up over the years at New Norcia by former students have been fantastic. A bond exists between people from different eras, due to the hardships met with, something everyone can relate to. 'Once a mission boy always a mission boy,' they say.

Trauma would have touched everyone's heart in their time at the mission, and even today I see young Aborigines pass on through such things as alcoholism, and I believe it is due to their past experiences.

However, the vision of the great man Salvado changed the whole aspect of Aborigines in the south-west of this State. From being outcast by the white settlers, they were offered some education to become working-class people, friendships, religious instruction and Catholic upbringing. A lot would have been lost without this intervention. The Aborigines owe much to his vision, teachings and aims.

I, for one, have made the transition to work in the Aboriginal community and to be respected in the white community. The days I spent at school and at work have given me the urge to continue to better myself and my family, and to work for my people who, I know, have suffered a great deal in the two hundred years of white settlement. I will always remember my time at New Norcia; the good times, the sad times; the people I met and the education I received. Independence, religious background, discipline and the ability to cope have been instilled in me for the long journey, enabling me to seek a better future for myself and for those I support.

THE COAT OF ARMS
OF THE ABBEY

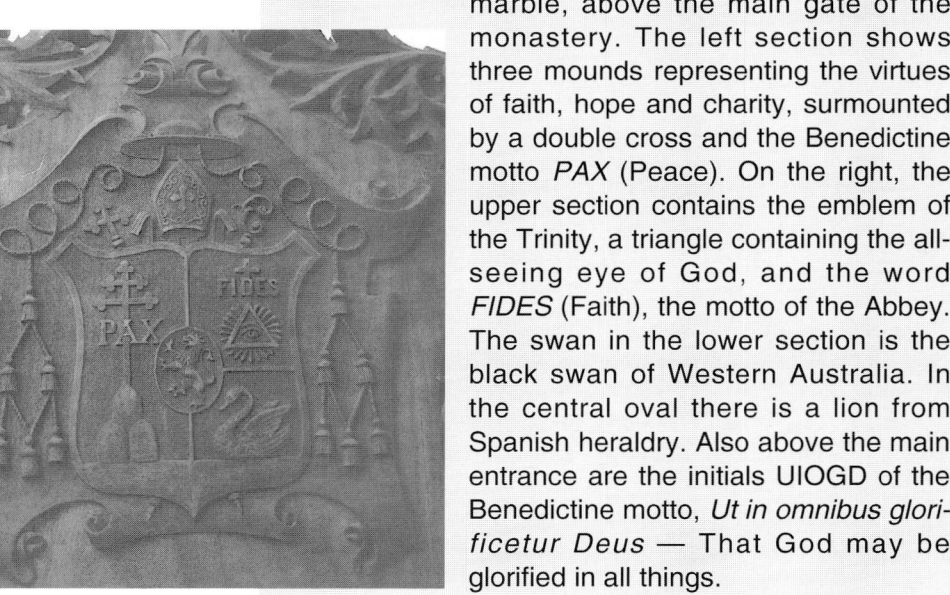

The coat of arms can be seen, carved in white marble, above the main gate of the monastery. The left section shows three mounds representing the virtues of faith, hope and charity, surmounted by a double cross and the Benedictine motto *PAX* (Peace). On the right, the upper section contains the emblem of the Trinity, a triangle containing the all-seeing eye of God, and the word *FIDES* (Faith), the motto of the Abbey. The swan in the lower section is the black swan of Western Australia. In the central oval there is a lion from Spanish heraldry. Also above the main entrance are the initials UIOGD of the Benedictine motto, *Ut in omnibus glorificetur Deus* — That God may be glorified in all things.

ABORIGINAL SPORTING TEAMS AT NEW NORCIA

The Aborigines took to Australian Rules football and cricket enthusiastically. Gabby Willaway, a former New Norcia pupil and sportsman, claims that sport 'really paved the way ... to equality between Aboriginal and white citizens of New Norcia'.

> Cricket ... I believe, started around about 1886 era when the then Lefroy, the Station Manager at Walebing, had gathered together a team of Aborigines from around the district, in particular New Norcia and Walebing ... and Moora ... they played the game locally against surrounding districts. Also I believe they'd played teams from the Perth area ... they'd travelled by horse and cart, taking them two to three days or more ...... The spirit of cricket in those days was to play the game, not really necessarily to win, and this attitude is shown in the sporting ways of the people around New Norcia in those days.[71]

> The city was new and strange to them ... Perth was there to a man. This time the native team lost the match. Fremantle had the crack team of the colony and laughed at the idea of a few black boys having a go against themselves, the champions. However, when the natives went to Fremantle and played the champions, the game resulted in an ignominious defeat for the Fremantlites.[72]

As the history of Australian Rules Football shows, the Aborigines have shown a special aptitude for this game; it was for a long time a favourite sport at New Norcia.

> One of the highlights was the establishment of the Central Midlands Association in 1961 ... We combined with the Moora Reserve and there were some young fellows that were available to play from the Mogumber Mission ... in the first year ... they took off the Grand Final. This was a controversial decision because it was the first time that an Aboriginal team had played in the Association even though there were always

Gabby Willaway with his sporting trophies, 1967.
[*Courtesy of Battye Library 74562P*]

Lefroy's first cricket team, 1879. Back row, from left : Paul Giater (Y'atter), Paddy Yappo, John Walley, Benedict Cuper*, Anthony Nelabut, Alex Wegnola, Felix Jackimara. Front row, from left: James Egaan, John Blurton (seated low), Henry (later Sir Henry) Lefroy, Frederick Yrbel, Joseph Nogolgot.

The second New Norcia cricket team. Standing, from left: Paul Giater, Frederick Yrbel, Charlie Ponang, John Walley, Henry Indich**, William Monap,*** Paddy Yappo. Seated, from left:, John Maher, Felix Jackimara, John Blurton, Mick Mendemara.

* Husband of the first Post Mistress at New Norcia;
**Trevor Walley's great grandfather — see p. 37;
*** See wedding photograph, p. 67

individual people playing for the numerous clubs around the time ...[73]

Teams from New Norcia travelled frequently to the Moore River Native Settlement for games of football and cricket, games played with spirited rivalry.

The Moore River Settlement football team was very skilled, but this didn't stop them feeling intimidated by their arch-rivals from nearby New Norcia. Ned Mippy recalls that the New Norcia boys would arrive by truck about once a month. 'We thought they were good,' Ned recalls, 'but we used to beat them.' The Moore River mob were keenly aware of the comparative affluence of the Catholic visitors: 'They had better school in there, and they did see butter on their bread. We used to say 'butter and bread comin' to play bread and scrape' ... They came there with ties on and everything and we didn't know what a tie was ... The behaviour of the settlement girls hardly helped matters. According to Ned, they would invariably barrack for the other side! Hazel Colbung Anderson confirms this, pointing out that the young people used the New Norcia games to score points in more ways than one: 'That's where some of them, some of the New Norcia boys, got in love with the settlement girls and they got married.'[74]

An account of a football match, between St Ildephonsus' College and Victoria Plains in the *Record* (18 August 1934) shows that florid prose is not new to sporting writers:

College were in an unassailable position at the commencement of the last term. They were eleven goals to the good, and seemed likely to increase the leeway. But a big shock was in store for all. Plains, with their backs to the wall, fought hard to avert defeat. G Clune, at centre half forward, rose splendidly to the occasion, and a long punt by the same player sent the twin flags waving. This effort put new heart into the team, and they set about overhauling College in a determined fashion. Through the instrumentality of G Clune, six goals were added in reply to College's two, but the lead was too big and the final bell announced the defeat, though certainly not the disgrace of Plains.

Harold and Philomena Willaway's wedding at Holy Trinity Church, New Norcia, 14 June 1944. Fr Bernard Escubano in the middle.
[*Courtesy of Battye Library 78098P*]

Harold Willaway and the St Mary's cricket team, 1966. [*Courtesy of Battye Library 72965P*]

Harold Willaway and the St Mary's football team, 1967. [*Courtesy of Battye Library 72964P*]

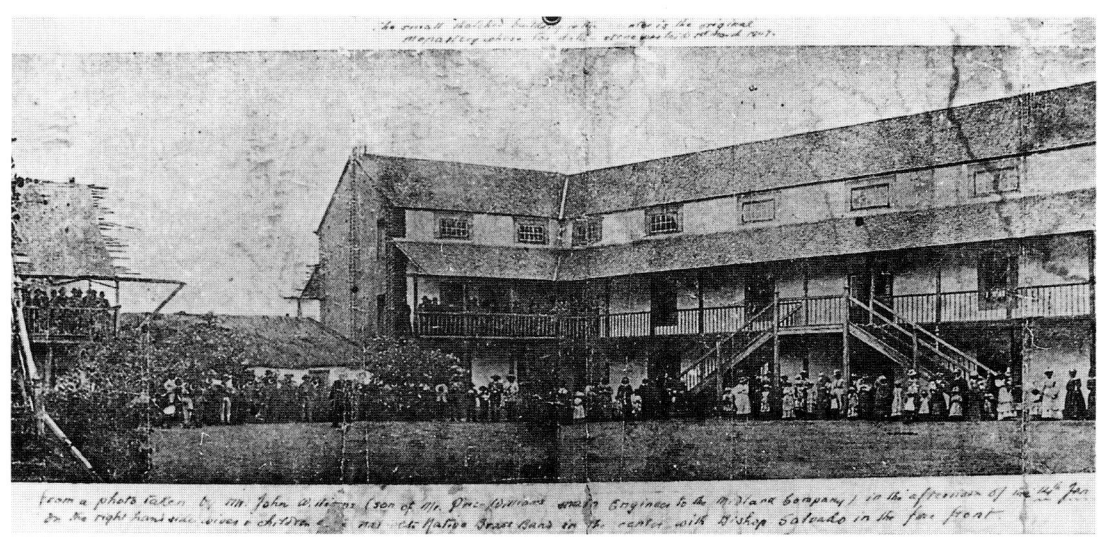

The Monastery, 14 January 1886.
[Courtesy of Battye Library 74903P]

Bishop Salvado (centre rear) and the Community, September 1893.
[Courtesy of Battye Library 66691P]

NEW NORCIA AFTER SALVADO

Nineteen ninety-six will be the sesquicentenary year of the Mission. For a little over a third of the first 150 years, the Community was led by Salvado. During the second third, the Spanish influence continued to predominate, under two Spanish Abbots, Fulgentius Torres and Anselm Catalan. In the final third of that period, firstly under the last Spanish Abbot, Gregory Gomez (1951–1971), that influence began to diminish; the Spanish language ceased to be the 'official' language. An Australian Abbot, Bernard Rooney (1974–1980) followed Gomez, and he has been succeeded by two Australian Priors, Father Justin Bruce (1980–1983) and Father Placid Spearritt (from 1983).

Dom Fulgentius Torres, 1903.
[Courtesy of Battye Library 73887P]

The history of New Norcia since Salvado has, so far, been less well-researched and is yet to be told in full. Salvado had the task of contacting and gaining the confidence of the Noongars and of founding the Mission. His successors had to consolidate monastic life and develop the physical support necessary for its maintenance. New directions had to be found when social changes, reflected in legislation, militated against the continuation of the Aboriginal mission.

Salvado's first choice as successor, Dom Fulgentius Dominguez, died while Salvado was on his final visit to Europe. Early in that visit, Salvado had met Dom Fulgentius Torres, to whom he extended the invitation to succeed him. Torres arrived at New Norcia in 1901 and was consecrated Bishop in 1910. He was a native of the Balearic Isles. When his family opposed his entry to monastic life he studied at the University of Barcelona, obtaining degrees in Arts and Science. Eventually, in 1885, he entered the Abbey of Montserrat. After ordination he spent some time teaching in the missionary college and was then sent to the Benedictine mission at Mindanao in the Philippines. At the outbreak of the Spanish-American war he returned to Europe, where Salvado met him. Apart from his formal studies, he gained some knowledge of music, medicine and architecture. The latter was to serve him well; he became the builder of New Norcia. Much of the fabric of the town as it now stands is due to him. Like Salvado, he was a polymath; in all his dealings he was considerate and gentle.

It is not surprising that much has been written about Salvado, a dominant figure for so long; he also had the more romantic role of pioneer. He was also a good observer and an entertaining and industrious writer. Torres' life was cut short and he was a more laconic writer than Salvado.[75]

Realising that the colonial missionary phase had ended, Torres adopted new policies and strategies energetically as soon as he was formally elected Abbot in 1902, moving quickly

to convert New Norcia from its mission organisation into something more like that of a regular monastery. Some of the older lay brothers, who had traditionally slept in the orchard or stables and dressed more like agricultural labourers than monks, were moved back under the monastery roof and into the Benedictine habit. The monastery itself was renovated and extended ...[76]

His changes were not readily accepted by all the monks who had spent the pioneering years with Salvado; nor were they in the wider community which believed that he was turning the Community inward and away from social responsibility.

Besides founding two colleges, he enlarged the Aboriginal orphanages, and made them more architecturally harmonious with the other buildings. He added the tower and new frontage to the Abbey Church. The Monastery library was remodelled. To achieve this building programme, he brought out skilled artisans and artists to work on the adornment of new and existing buildings. They included the woodcarver layman, John Casellas, and the artists Dom Lesmes and Brother Salvador. Their work, and that of the musician Dom Stephen Moreno, are dealt with elsewhere.

In 1903, the area of the Abbey Nullius was extended greatly. In 1905, the Third

A SILVER MEDAL FOR OLIVE OIL

The Franco British Exhibition
London, 22 October 1908

Dear Sir,

I have the honour to inform you that you have been awarded a Diploma for Silver Medal for your exhibit of Olive Oil at the Franco British Exhibition.

We are unable at the present time to give the actual cost but the probability is that the Silver Medal will be £3-3-0.

I shall be glad if you will kindly advise me by return mail c/o the Agent General for Western Australia, 15 Victoria Street, Westminster, as to whether you would like us to obtain this medal for you.

Yours faithfully
Percy G. Wicken
Officer in Charge

(At the same Exhibition the Monastery was awarded the Gold Medal for macaroni.)

The Hostel (now Hotel) under construction, c1927.
[*Courtesy of Battye Library 74217P*]

Back view of the Monastery, 1940.
[*Courtesy of Battye Library 72833P*]

Plenary Council of the Australian Hierarchy invited Torres to undertake a new mission in the north-west. In the following year he led an exploration of the Kimberley for a suitable site; finally selecting one on the Drysdale River (at Pago; it was later moved to Kalumburu). The foundation was approved in 1910.

Torres must have overtaxed himself. After his second visit to the Kimberley in 1908 for the foundation of the Drysdale River Mission, his health failed. He died on 5 October 1914.

The next Abbot, Anselm Catalan, remained in office for thirty-five years. He was born in Corella, Navarre, in 1878 and entered Montserrat Monastery in 1892, being ordained in 1901. Like Torres, he spent time in the Philippines, where he was a teacher and eventually President at St Bede's College, Manila. In 1914, he was appointed Abbot Visitor of the Benedictine Abbeys of the Spanish Province. The first place he had to visit was New Norcia, to supervise the election of Torres' successor. To his surprise — and consternation — he was himself elected on 27 March 1916, and confirmed by the Holy See in June. He had wished to spend the rest of his life at Montserrat but, apart from some visits to Europe and the north-west, he was to spend it at New Norcia. He retired in 1951 and died eight years later.

His period was one of transition, and during it two world wars and the Depression must have affected the Monastery life considerably. He continued the work of his predecessor in developing the monastic and liturgical life, without any major changes in policy. He stabilised the Mission property, the buildings and the farming equipment. He had modern machinery installed in the workshops and an electrical plant. Bookbinding equipment and a medium-sized printing press were acquired. The building programme of this period is detailed elsewhere. He gave new impetus to the Drysdale River Mission and encouraged Dom Moreno to

THE MISSING KEYS

(From a letter to Abbot Catalan from Fr. Ruiz, 31 March 1922)

Here I send your Lordship a brief account of the most important events that have happened during your absence. First of all, about the keys in the 'old trousers'. Rumour had it here that we were called 'some names' because 'we did not look for the keys in the place we were told to look at' and many other things — not very pleasant — in the same key, concerning the lost keys. I have to explain what happened, if an explanation is necessary at all. Br. Joseph took the 'trousers' to the laundry as soon as your Lordship left the Monastery — He goes to serve the 5 o'c Mass. When we were told to look for the keys in the 'old trousers' — we looked at every 'old trousers' — there are about six — in your room. Naturally enough the keys were nowhere to be found. The very day that your Lordship sailed for Manila, Br. Joseph came all triumphantly with the keys. Sr Mary had found them in the pocket of your Lordship's trousers — but, unfortunately, it was too late! This is the simple story of the 'keys in the old trousers'. You see, then, that we are not to blame.

Bishop Torres in Cape and Mitre, c1910.
[*Courtesy of Battye Library 73625P*]

Abbot Catalan and the German flier, Hans Bertram, 1932.

Bertram and his fellow aviator, Adolph Klausman, were on a demonstration flight of a Junkers seaplane when they were forced, by a storm, to put down on the Kimberley coast on 15 May 1932. Completely lost, they failed in several attempts to walk for help, and then made a canoe out of the stern half of one of the aircraft's floats in which they attempted to travel. Close to death — they had been without food for forty days — they were dis-covered by an Aboriginal search party from the Drysdale River Mission.

The improvised canoe is in the Western Australian Maritime Museum, Fremantle.

[*Courtesy of Battye Library 72698P*]

develop music at the Monastery, and the artistic work of Father Lesmes and John Casellas, and acquired many of the European paintings in the art collection. By sending young Spanish monks to study at the Manly Seminary in Sydney he initiated the process of 'Australianisation' which accelerated under his successors.

Dom Gregory Gomez was elected to succeed Catalan in October 1951. Although Western Australia was shortly to enter a second major mineral boom, for the Monastery it was a period of contraction. The most important of his achievements was the increasing involvement of Australian monks in the administration. The area of the diocese was reduced substantially by the handing over of its largest parish, Southern Cross, to the Perth Archdiocese. The Benedictine Community took over St Ildephonsus' College when the Marists withdrew. The English language was gradually introduced into the mass and the Divine Office. Many New Norcia buildings were updated and extended.

When Abbot Gomez retired in 1971, Dom Bernard Rooney was appointed Prior-Administrator, and was then elected Abbot in 1974 — the fifth Abbot, but the first Australian in the position. Contraction of the diocese continued, with the handing over of other parishes to Perth in the early 1970s. The two colleges were merged as the coeducational Salvado College, and the Museum and Art Gallery were established. Abbot Rooney retired in 1980 to devote himself to helping the Aborigines of the area to reconnect with their own culture.

During the short period of Prior Justin Bruce's term as Superior (1980–1983) and under his successor, Father Placid Spearritt, the Community has had to face many new and sometimes taxing issues, as the latter has outlined in his article. The Benedictines withdrew from the Drysdale River Mission in 1982. Salvado College was closed in 1991. However, there has been an extensive building programme: the original 'temporary' Chapel has been replaced with the new Chapel above the Lower Guest House; the Upper Guest House was completed. A new wing, adding twelve bedrooms for monastic accommodation was also built.

As it approaches its sesquicentenary, the Monastery has been affected by a major recession which has reduced the farm income. The society of Western Australia is also changing rapidly again. Once again new directions must be found for the Community; no doubt it will succeed in this challenge, as it has done so before. The central purpose remains the same: to follow the Rule of St Benedict.

AN EASTER VISITOR, 1919

A visitor from Perth, Mr J G Hay, spent Easter 1919 at New Norcia, staying in the Hostel. He took up two pages of the Hostel's Visitors' Book[77] to record his enjoyment of all that New Norcia had to offer:

> Today, I have had the added privilege of seeing those fine monuments of Education that would have gladdened [Salvado's] eyes. Perhaps, the most striking feature about the buildings is the prodigality of the excellent paintings of the local monk (Fr Lesmes), whose work I venture to assert is not equalled throughout the whole Commonwealth of Australia — whether it be in mural decoration or massive paintings of Benedictine Saint or other religious subject. I trust this Fra Angelico will long be spared the community. In other Art decoration may be mentioned the good work of carving of a layman here.
>
> Another great asset of this monastery is the invaluable collection of works, particularly of Patristic Theology, some of which are unique, and could not be replaced if lost, or destroyed.
>
> But to me, one of the greatest charms of the institution is the entrancing style of music adopted in the Church Service. Starting from an ordinary low tone the sudden transition of forte to fortissimo pitch, and as suddenly descending similarly, has a startling and arrestive effect in the hearer. The rhythmic melody is further punctuated by the recurring pause of a second or two between chords. For want of a more exact term I should call this music a florid Gregorian chant.
>
> The Rule of Benedict inculcates teaching, and the two fine buildings whether the massive erection of St Ildephonsus' in Byzantine architecture for boys, or the Spanish Gothic college of St Gertrude's for the girls, are eloquent evidence of the Catholic spirit here existing. I trust the sacrificing work of the Marist Brothers for the boys, and equally good efforts of the Sisters of St Joseph for the girls, will bear, in the days to come, fruit to verify the Benedictine objective, *Ut in omnibus glorificetur Deus*.
>
> The well-known hospitality of the Benedictine, the oldest religious order of Western Europe, needs no comment from me, and I can only wish for the courteous Lord Abbot of the community, Dom Anselm Catalan, and his valuable adjunct, the manager, Father Castanares,
>
> *Ad multos annos*.

Abbot Gregory Gomez, c1951. Abbot Gregory was tragically killed in a car accident, in 1995, at the age of ninety-one.
[Courtesy of Battye Library 72805P]

Father Justin Bruce, Prior 1980–1983.

NOONGAR, WINDJAR KURL?*:
CULTURAL AWARENESS —
A CHALLENGE FOR THE NINETIES[78]

ABBOT BERNARD ROONEY, OSB

Bishop Salvado, unlike most of his contemporaries, saw the value of the Australian indigenous culture. From the inception of his mission, he set about learning the language, lifestyle and culture of the Noongar people. It was then more fashionable, even among missionaries, to despise and reject Aboriginal culture, seeking to replace it with the 'higher values' of the Old World. He also saw the darker side of that culture and sought to modify the harsh penalties, including death, imposed for breaches of the law. He deplored the harsh treatment of women, including the practice of putting to death at birth every third female child, and other practices.

During the early years of settlement, the Aborigines were dispossessed, victimised and killed. Then the settlers found the Noongar useful in helping to clear land, to shepherd stock, and as labourers. The Aborigines were able to remain near their lands and to maintain much of their age-old culture.

Till the turn of the century, a large number of Noongars lived at the Mission, by far the greatest number of them at New Norcia. After 1900, however, the clearing of vast areas of crown land, extensive fencing, and intensive cultivation, contributed to a marked deterioration in Aboriginal social conditions and cultural life. The Noongar people suffered social discrimination and physical segregation. They found less employment and were denied access to their lands, and were forced to live in reserves on the fringes of towns and cities, denied even the most basic human freedoms. Their children were taken from them and placed in settlements.

Many whites believed that the Aborigines would die out, or be forced to assimilate. With their culture so diminished, the first Australians lost their identity and self-esteem, becoming alienated from an alien society.

In 1974, as Abbot, I saw our Institution for Aboriginal children forced to close. The older generation of Noongar people had long been encouraged to make a life for themselves elsewhere. The only people remaining were the families of those employed at New Norcia. By the mid-1970s, after 130

---

* Noongar, where are you going? (The spelling of Noongar is variable. In Moora, it is usually rendered as 'Nyungar')

years of dedication to the Aboriginal cause, New Norcia ceased to be a mission.

I often wondered what could be done to assist the Aboriginal community. New Norcia had unfinished business; it could not easily turn its back on more than a century of Aboriginal ministry.

I wondered what Salvado, given our hindsight, would have done. He founded a mission where the people could live, work, own their land, and maintain their lifestyle and social relationships, insulated to some extent from the harmful influences and injustices of the white man's world. He established 'orphanages', where the children could imbibe a Christian and Catholic faith and be prepared, through education, for life in the wider community. It was a noble vision, unmatched by any of his missionary contemporaries. For a time it worked; but what of the future?

The Faith had been presented in the garb of Old Europe, and did not speak to the people through their own culture. The education was that of a white man; it told them nothing of their identity, and prepared them for a life which was out of reach of most of them. They were sent out into a world unwilling to receive them, where their parents, family and friends lived on reserves, in the fringes of towns and in the ghettos of cities.

One thing was clear; no latter-day Salvado would found another mission like the nineteenth century New Norcia. An entirely new approach was required. In 1981, I committed myself to finding out the needs of the Noongar community. I made regular pastoral visits to the Alcohol Rehabilitation Project at Wandering, to Ken Colbung's Noongar Community at Gnangara, to the Cullacabardie Village, as well as to individuals in Perth and Moora.

Across the whole social spectrum I found extreme disadvantage: poor health, reduced life expectancy, lack of proper hygiene and nutrition, lack of respect for the education system, almost universal unemployment, and almost universal excessive drinking. This was a demoralised people, dispossessed not only of their land and society, but of their very identity. Without a reaffirmation of culture, of personal identity, no combination of government handouts, welfare programmes, voting rights, land rights, and suchlike, could raise the morale and expectations of a socially depressed people.

By the early 1980s, Aborigines throughout Australia could take no more, and time was ripe for change in this State. In 1984, I considered myself well placed to contribute to the re-awakening of Aboriginal culture. Without such a reawakening, the downward spiral would continue and end in the destruction of an entire race and culture.

In 1981, I met a man who, I am sure, was put in my way by

Abbot Bernard Rooney and Lester Jacobs, a New Norcia farmhand, on a four-wheeled motorcycle, 1993.
[Courtesy of West Australian Newspapers]

Divine Providence: Edward Mippy, known to me as 'Ned', a true Elder of his people. He was to be for me both a kindred spirit and an indispensable mentor in the ways and traditions of the people I felt called to serve. With him, I studied the Noongar language, and learned much of the traditions and lore of his people.

In 1984, at my request, I was appointed to the Parish of Moora, which has the highest percentage of Noongar inhabitants of any town in the south-west. By then I had a good working knowledge of the Yuat dialect of the Noongar language. With Ned's assistance, and the enthusiastic support of the Sisters of St Joseph, I started a pilot programme in the

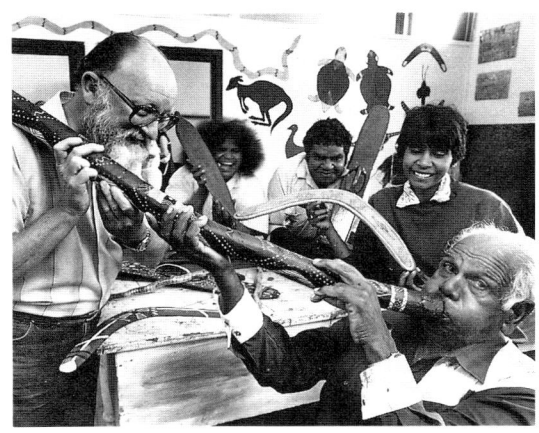

Ned Mippy tests a newly-made didgeridoo for Abbot Bernard Rooney, 1991.

[*Courtesy of West Australian Newspapers*]

language at St Joseph's Primary School, where sixty per cent of the pupils were Aboriginal. This became part of the school curriculum; the first ever formal education programme in the Noongar language. It became a favourite with all the children, Aboriginal and non-Aboriginal. It was a shock to some Aboriginal parents, and there was an initial negative reaction in some quarters. However, for them, it reaffirmed strongly that their language was a vital part of their inheritance. Some white parents realised that the language and culture of the first Australians had significant value for all Australians: a unique national resource.

In addition to language, the children were introduced to Aboriginal arts and crafts, with the cooperation of the Central Midlands Senior High School, where the woodwork department was made available. This programme is now established permanently at St Joseph's, in their own woodwork centre. Under Ned's tutelage, the children learned to identify local traditional bush foods, and were enthralled by Dreamtime stories which he related in his inimitable style.

In the bush near the Presbytery, a corroboree ground was built with voluntary labour. Here the Noongar children were taught to perform their own dances, and the youth of Moora played host to visiting dance groups from all over the State, including the Perth professional Noongar group, the Midar. Some of the dances are still performed at school concerts and other venues.

Another concern was the lack of Aboriginal involvement with the Church. Ned, who was not a Catholic, constructed a group of maya-mayas. Here, on Sundays, the Moora people, most of them Catholic, assembled to take part in an open-air Mass followed by a feast of whole kangaroo or emu, baked in an authentic earth oven, and lashings of Mission bread. Sometimes these occasions were enlivened by a youth corroboree. The 'camp fire masses' became very popular.

Employment opportunities were created in the old Church Hall: a spinning and weaving programme lasted for a year until it was wound up through lack of finance. A second project, paper-bark painting, also fell on hard times. So, in 1988, remembering that Salvado had two unsuccessful attempts before establishing his mission, I tried a third time. The Aboriginal artefacts project at St Joseph's had proved so popular with the children I saw that it could be extended to adults. Ned and I formed a traditional arts and crafts group under the local Noongar name 'YUAT'. With the help of a donation, I set up the hall with woodworking machines and tools, and invited locals to rediscover their traditional crafts and skills, under the tutelage of reliable Ned.

It took some time for the idea to catch on. Doomsayers said it would come to nothing: why should people on the dole work? Thanks be to God, they were wrong. The Department of Employment, Education and Training provided a comprehensive, fully-funded training scheme, with an ongoing scheme for the paid employment of several trainees working four days a week. The people worked enthusiastically, eventually developing their own techniques and art forms, and their own Dreamtime logo. YUAT Artefacts is now established, permanently funded under the CDEP programme, and provides employment for a dozen men and women. The programme has been extended to Mogumber and throughout the wheatbelt.

After my return to New Norcia in 1988, I became a part-time teacher in Aboriginal Studies with the Moora division of TAFE Aboriginal Access, and an accredited tutor in Aboriginal Studies at the High School and, later, part-time teacher in Noongar language when that subject was incorporated in the regular secondary Aboriginal Studies curriculum.

To further the programme, YUAT Cultural Awareness, a committee of Noongar people, was established to look at the problems of juvenile delinquency, one of Moora's major problems. Funding was obtained from the Department of Community Development, the Lotteries Commission and other sources, to organise outings and excursions for Noongar youth, many of whom were disadvantaged and more or less chronic offenders.

Regular daily or weekend excursions for recreation became very popular. We have also tried to organise one major excursion per year to various remote Aboriginal communities, as far afield as the Santa Teresa Mission, the home of the Eastern Arrente people south-east of Alice Springs.

None of this would have been possible without the moral and practical support of Ned Mippy. His death on 5 May 1992, after a short illness, was a terrible shock for us all. His seventy-three years of unremitting work in the service of his people continues to be a source of pride, not only to his family and many descendants, but to all those who share the fruits of his labours. He had been awarded the 1991 Advance Australia Award.

THE WORD

Faye Davis

8 Nov: Mrs Cuper came to tell me that she had two
telegrams for the Leader of an expedition which had
arrived from Adelaide at Mr Clark's. Finding herself
on her own, she did not know what to do with them, by
whom to send them, or where. Immediately I got
Henry and Freddy to get ready, and at 2 pm they set
out on horseback, each with a duplicate of the
telegrams, Freddy to go to Mr Clark's place, and Henry
to go to Mr Lefroy's; in this way, if they don't find the
members of the expedition in one place, they will find
them in the other ...[79]

Across a continent they came, traversing east to west, across
desert, wave upon wave of sand, by ridge and rock outcrop,
through scrub so dense the man records: 'the country ...
filled to overflowing with the densest of scrubs; Nature
seemed to have tried how much of it she could possibly jam
into this region.' Lake bed after lake bed will hem them in,
force them to circumnavigate, to press on, forever fearful of
the animals becoming trapped in the saline depressions. At
times ridge or sheer outcrop in an ancient region forces alter-
nate courses through the most tenacious vegetation. The land
dry, so dry the man will write: 'perhaps it has not rained for
a year' and, desperate, 'or is it a hundred?' But the men will
push forward, toward some hill, some horizon, to contem-
plate, to puzzle at, sometimes to despair, for at times the
spectacle will be 'enough to terrify the spectator.' And,
however enduring, there is their need for water, always to be
searched for, and their need for food. That day, the explorer
will write, they 'eat lowan's eggs,' eggs from 'the birds that
swarm here in the desert scrub.'

And the party will come upon natives and, thankfully for
them, native wells; the man to describe the wells in his
journal. He will record, too, evidence of the natives' surprise
at the quantity of water consumed by the strange animals
brought across the desert by these white men, for these men
have entered an unknown region, the ways of which are
strange to them. They bring with them no knowledge of
when the wells will be replenished. But the man will record

in his journal his attitude towards a native guide, who leads them to a place where he remembers there is water. The explorer is 'struck with admiration at his having done so at all, and how he or any other human being, not having the advantage of science ... could possibly return to the places ... visited in such a wilderness.'

The explorer describes, too, the ingenious traps made by the natives to catch wallaby. Once, we will read, when in the Gibson Desert, he himself had fallen with unforgettable gratitude on a small dying wallaby, lately thrown from its mother's pouch, and devoured it 'fur, skin, bones, skull and all.' For it is only in the passed-on word that we know such things, for the desert will destroy all evidence as will time itself.

By night the party encamps, both men and their beasts come to rest. In the strange way of the desert, the intense cold will penetrate beyond imagining in the stark heat of day. Often, beneath a vast sky, the man reflects upon his journey, and, in this solitude, on the journey of mankind, for he is a reflective man, and diligent. He records, however arduous the day's journey, the names of plants and trees: mallee, mulga, bloodwood, yellow-barked eucalyptus, the grass tree Xanthorrhea, casuarina, and quandong; and write in detail of the magenta-coloured vetch; of the scarlet flower of Sturt's desert pea, noting its botanical name, *Clianthus formosus*, given long before Sturt; of the dreaded triodia; the dull-green samphire, the cliff plant with aromatic, saline fleshy leaves. He records the grevillea (or beefwood tree) upon which they indent the explorer's initials and the numerals 1875, a strange concept of history in a prehistoric land, for man brings with him his own concepts. Though, by whatever means time is measured, it passes. Soon the party will come out of the wilderness, so suddenly in fact that they are surprised — and surprise the lone horseman.

They will come, too, upon an outlying station, 'its buildings consisting simply of a few bark gunyahs.' At a remote farm the men from the east will be provided with butter and eggs, even jam and spirits. The man records in his journal: 'Exploring had now come to an end; roads led to, and from, all the other settled districts of the colony, and we were in the neighbourhood of civilisation once more.'

So it came to pass, for it is written, that the party came then upon 'a Spanish Benedictine Monastery and Home for Natives, called New Norcia.' We can wonder then at the feelings on that day in November when they reached the monastic settlement displaying both Spanish ardour and architecture. After such a journey, to come to a monastery, the church, a mill, stables, a little house, and scattered buildings that comprised a visionary settlement. 'Here,' the man will record 'was the first telegraph station we had reached,' and 'I received ... telegrams ... from His Excellency the Governor's private secretary, the Press and my brother-explorer Mr John Forrest.' Invitations flowed in to attend receptions, the first of which was at the Monastery itself.

> 9 Nov: Henry and Freddy returned from Walebing with a telegram from Mr Giles who, they say, will come here tomorrow with his party.
> 10 Nov.: Eleven flags were put in position and the shooters made ready to fire salvos at the arrival of the explorers ... but they stopped at McPherson's house to sleep ...[80]

However, on the following day,

> 11 Nov: Shortly before midday Mr Ernest Giles ... arrived with his explorer companions, i.e. seven persons ... and eighteen camels, large and small. They then took refreshments, and dined at 1.00 pm. At 6.00 pm they again took refreshments, had supper at 8.00 pm and went to bed at 10.00 pm.
> 12 Nov.: ... the explorers went to wash and bathe at the pool rather early ... they breakfasted at 8.00 and left at 9.30.[81]

The party would have been anxious to complete the final stages of their journey. They had crossed the continent to reach the Swan River Colony, but it must have been with considerable regret that they farewelled the monks and members of the community that morning. The monks had brought their particular influence from a distant culture, and there would be much to share and exchange between men. Whatever friendships were made were lasting, for it is known that Ernest Giles was to return. Following the departure of the party that morning, the explorer would record that the Monastery 'was presided over by the Right Reverend Lord Bishop Salvado, the kindest and most urbane of holy fathers.' However valuable solitude or silence, it is only through the word that we have such knowledge: the word recorded, or passed down from generation to generation, tribe to tribe, in rite or lore, in a letter home, a diary, a journal diligently kept.[82]

Electric Telegraph, West Australia.

New Norcia Jan. 24th 1876.

TIME 12.30 P.M.

BY H. Cooper

The following Telegram received here from Newcastle
Station, subject to the Regulations and Conditions printed on the other side:—

TO The Lord Bishop Salvado
New Norcia

Dear Father, I hope to
have the pleasure of reaching
your establishment on
Wednesday —

Ernest Giles
Newcastle

A telegram sent by Ernest Giles from Newcastle (Toodyay) to
Bishop Salvado during his return journey.

THE FIRST NEW NORCIA POSTMISTRESS

In the early 1870s Perth and Geraldton were connected by telegraph and a Post Office and Telegraph Station was erected at New Norcia. Mary Ellen Pangieran (Cuper) was selected to be the telegraphist. She was trained in morse telegraphy by Father Coll, who combined teaching with his duties as Dispensing Chemist. Bishop Salvado took a personal interest in Mrs Cuper's training. She took up her position as telegraphist and Postmistress in 1874. After only three years in this office, she contracted tuberculosis. Before she died, in February 1877 aged only 30 years, she had trained another woman, Sarah, to take over. Her deeply grieving husband had a special tombstone erected over her grave, on which is engraved the story of her life.

Mary Helen Pangieran (Mrs Cuper), the first Post Mistress at New Norcia, c1875.
[*Courtesy of Battye Library 73397P*]

A LETTER FROM LORD CARNARVON TO GOVERNOR ROBINSON

Sir,

I have the honour to acknowledge the receipt of your Despatch No 9 of 20th of January enclosing a photograph of 'Sarah' a pure-bred aboriginal who has been acting as Postmistress and Telegraph Operator at the New Norcia Station in Western Australia.

The intelligence displayed by this woman in the execution of her duties reflects great credit on the manner in which the natives are trained and cared for at Bishop Salvado's Mission.

I have the honour to be Sir,
Your most obedient humble servant

Carnarvon

NEW NORCIA IN HISTORY: CHANGING THE FRAME[83]

Tom Stannage

The most potent of the major traditions of interpretation of history in and about Australia is modern British historical writing, which was devised to help define Englishness and to validate and serve the British Empire.

The historians who founded this approach believed that constitutionalism and the freedom of the people were found in English mediaeval and modern history. History would be literary, scientific and undergirded by Anglican Christianity, by English language and literature. It would have a moral purpose: to bear the idea of progress. The English gifts, so defined, should be carried to the world, especially to the Empire. By the turn of the century, the practice of history had become a branch of Empire statesmanship.

Australian historians, such as Fred Alexander and Sir Keith Hancock, published works in the 1930s which evoked just this historiographical line: English, Protestant, Christian, male, and imbued with racial superiority, powerfully linked to the idea of progress which undergirded the British Empire. The British people were seen to be the most socially efficient and, therefore, had the right to rule. This sort of thinking led to 'Social Darwinism', an 'inexorable law of natural selection' which would result in the extermination of 'the inferior Australian and Maori races' and the world would be 'the better for it'.

This tradition dominated history and historical interpretation and presentation in Western Australia; within it New Norcia, particularly Bishop Salvado's New Norcia, could sit comfortably. Thus the Protestant Westralian, James Sykes Battye, the State's principal librarian and historian, could praise Salvado, along with other pastoralists, businessmen and churchmen, as apostles of free enterprise and Empire. In 1977, late in the life of this tradition, Geoffrey Bolton wrote empathically about Salvado in Father Stormon's edition of the *Salvado Memoirs*. Midway between Battye and Bolton lies Sir Hal Colebatch's edited *A Story of a Hundred Years*, published in 1929.

> The story of one hundred years cannot fail to be inspiring. Few colonising enterprises have been embarked upon in the face of greater natural difficulties — none has resulted in more complete success ... Western Australia has become the home of a happy and prosperous people, full of love and patriotism for 'their country and of confidence in its resources'.

Chapters of this book move through the trials of the early settlers, exploration and the establishment of British civilisation, through politics, self-government, etc. It is a success story of patriotism, confidence and courage. One chapter, 'The Aborigines', written by A O Neville, Protector of Aborigines, is an equally happy story of a movement from savagery, nudity, stone-ageness, and simpleness. As a people they 'gave way' before the white men, and became decadent despite the best efforts of Government and latterly the Aborigines Department. 'The work of the department is ably seconded by the various missionary societies,' wrote Neville.

There is also a chapter, 'A bit of Old Spain', by an unknown author, possibly Abbot Catalan. It is a hymn of praise to 'pioneering', with early difficulties overcome by energy and courage, patience and efficiency. Key phrases are 'toil and heroism', 'the mission grew rapidly', 'always his thought was for the natives', 'his magnetic personality ... attracted to him men of all creeds'. The final lines of this chapter read:

> This Benedictine settlement stands without rival as a place of downright interest, as a centre of artistic and architectural attraction and as an example of the complete conquest of pioneering hardships.

From the 1960s there were major historiographical changes. There were the voices not only of social justice and freedom through service to Empire but also of social justice through self-determination and the rights of minorities and marginalised groups. In the late 1960s and 1970s it was youthful rebellion, a rejection of Englishmen, England, Empireness, decay and disaster. It shouted a new role for history: for women, environment, black rights and the like. We must understand the past in order to destroy it.

That is what we have been doing for the past twenty years. Is a twenty-year battle ending in victory, or is it ending without victors and with the trade of history weakened, uncertain of its mission, unable to go back (as the New Right wants), ineffective, a servant of what? Does anyone care? I tire rather of the sound of hate and conflict. I search back across time to hear the voice of joy, however doused it seems by the voice of sorrow. I puzzle over evidence of happiness in the lives of the people of the past. We have been better with sorrow than with joy these past twenty years: better with human unhappiness than happiness.

The writing of Aboriginal history, women's history, the history of childhood, the oppressive nature of class relations, the ills of capitalism, the wretchedness of pastoralism and farming re the environment, the dangers of Anglo-Celtism, etc.; we have dwelt historiographically in a dark land.

From the mid 1980s, I began to worry greatly about the direction

I had gone. But there were momentous battles still raging, and one's emotions were still too deeply engaged. In 1987, my paper to the History Teachers Association National Conference was called 'The Sins of Omission'.

But to return to the historiography of New Norcia. Why was Russo's 1980 book, *Lord Abbot of the Wilderness*, so defensive about Salvado? C D Rowley in *The Destruction of Aboriginal Society*, offers some clues. He wrote of New Norcia, 'No mission effort to the Aboriginal has been so long sustained, and possibly none for a more meagre continuing reward'. Missions were ineffective, he wrote. This is not so much hostile towards New Norcia as sad; but the title was indicative. From this and from Aboriginal writers, New Norcia became a footnote in the world historical experience of racial oppression and exploitation, a very powerful frame of analysis, linked to rejection of Empire.

Then there is feminist history. What of New Norcia in this 'frame'? Women *were* present at New Norcia. There were the public/private lives of nuns, workers, students and others. What of the variants of the older left traditions? The new social history was hostile to the old left Roman Catholic history. The 1970s 'history from below' frame made New Norcia look very odd indeed, or bypassed it.

Even modern masculinist history may probe New Norcia in new ways which could horrify many people. And what of post-structuralism and New Norcia? And where does this leave New Norcia in relation to a restatement of the old Empire model — the New Right use of heritage? Does New Norcia retreat into an internalised and locked frame? I don't have a clear answer. I think the essence of New Norcia's historiographical response is to be found in the internalised experience, less of religious history generally, than of Benedictinism itself.

It begins with St Benedict about 450–543; it begins at Norcia, Subiaco, Monte Cassino; it begins with the Rule; it begins with the laymen and black monks; it begins with the idea of community, with labour and obedience; it begins with the experience of this and the refinements through to and beyond, at New Norcia, the December 1984 'Statement of Purpose' of the Benedictine Community of the Holy Trinity Abbey. It begins with fidelity to monastic life, to prayer and work, to silence and to service. It recognises that the community exists for the glory of God.

If it begins this way, it will help Australians to redefine themselves in spiritual terms. For here is a new frame, less of analysis, perhaps, than of faith, that can stand in relation to, and in contact with all the other frames of reference or analysis that I have pursued here. It can enlarge all these frames and remain true to itself. It cannot ignore these frames or it will not be listened to, and New Norcia will disappear down the historical drain of heritage — quaint, nostalgic, nothing to offer the future.

The next history of New Norcia must be spiritually bound, intellectually aggressive and socially assured.

What a challenge.

St Gertrude's College, c1910.
[*Courtesy of Battye Library 74111P*]

St Ildephonsus' College, 1970s.
[*Courtesy of Battye Library 74112P*]

THE COLLEGES OF NEW NORCIA

When the area of the Abbey Nullius was increased in 1903, the Catholic population in that area was only 1500. However, the closer settlement of the wheatbelt made it likely that the Victoria Plains would become more closely settled.[84] So, among the new directions which Torres brought to New Norcia was the foundation of two colleges for the education of white children: St Ildephonsus' for boys and St Gertrude's for girls.

A study of the history of St Ildephonsus' has some application to St Gertrude's as well.

> St Ildephonsus' provides ... a remarkably pure example of a Catholic secondary school in what might fairly be termed the 'epic' or 'heroic' age of Catholic education in Australia. By the time S.I.C. was founded, the 'Free, Compulsory and Secular' education controversies of the late nineteenth century had subsided ... All the colonial governments had withdrawn state financial supports from church schools, but the Catholic bishops, for their part, had succeeded too in convincing their flocks of the necessity and value of Catholic schools. Not just typically, but almost universally, these schools were single-sex, entirely staffed by, and virtually identified with, the religious teaching orders. Throughout its history, S.I.C. fitted this model precisely and it ceased to operate just as the theological upheaval of Vatican II in Europe and the introduction of Commonwealth financial assistance in Australia were beginning to make alternative models imaginable and economically possible.[85]

Both schools were affected by isolation and the monastic milieu. St Ildephonsus' in particular was

> ... almost absolutely isolated by the still rudimentary scope of mass media, by its geographic location ... and by the monastic atmosphere of the New Norcia Mission itself.[86]

An inscription on the marble slab at the entrance to St Gertrude's tells us that it was founded 'with a view to the upbringing in the Christian Religion of the Girls of Australia.' This suggests that it was intended for the education of Aboriginal girls. They were the first occupants of the college.[87] However, if this is what the Abbot intended, he must have reconsidered, because he opened St Gertrude's as a college for

Altar by John Casellas and murals by Fr Lesmes
in St Gertrude's College Chapel, before 1965.
[*Courtesy of Battye Library 74353P*]

white girls. He drew the plans for both colleges, having them checked by a Spanish architect, and supervised the building of them by the monks.[88]

Torres sought the help of Mother Mary McKillop (recently beatified), Founder of the Order of St Joseph, to provide teaching Sisters for New Norcia. In 1904, four Sisters were sent to teach at Southern Cross. In 1907, Torres requested more Sisters to staff St Gertrude's, and three were sent at the beginning of 1908. One of them, Sr Fintan, recorded their arrival.

Towards the end of January, 1908, Sisters Aelred, Norbert and Fintan travelled by train to Adelaide and from there to ... Fremantle, by boat ... arriving there on the 2nd February. We were met ... by Srs M. Julia, Ita, Carmel (Moore), Aloysia (Bridgewood) ... From there we went to Perth and stayed with a Catholic family — Coffee Palace — just at the back of the railway station. We stayed there till the following Friday when Srs Aelred, Carmel, Norbert and Aloysia left by the mail train for Southern Cross. On Saturday morning Sisters Julia, Ita, and Fintan left for New Norcia ... at Mogumber the Bishop's carriage was waiting ... We were taken to St Gertrude's and Bishop Torres welcomed us and left us in charge of ten Spanish Nuns (Teresians) who had the top part of the Convent where the Sisters' kitchen is now ... we rarely saw them except at Mass ... Those Sisters knew scarcely any English. They looked after the Native girls (about fifty in number) ... As we were at lunch some of the Native girls passed along, and this is the extent of the Spanish Nun's English, the girls looked in, and one of the Sisters said to the girls 'Shut up', she thought it was the right thing to say ...[89]

Teaching at the College started in 1908, with one boarder and a few day girls. By September the enrolment was thirty. The primary emphasis was on religious education, but there was also emphasis on academic excellence. The peak enrolment, 112, was reached in 1912.

Torres was generous, but St Gertrude's was stark, austere,

and hardly feminine. For the first fifty years the physical conditions did not change; for the first sixty years there was no heating or cooling. Internal toilets and water for personal ablutions were not available upstairs until the late 1950s.

Because of limited staff, there was a heavy load of teaching and chores; an almost impossible physical demand on the Sisters. Chores included laundering, cleaning, chopping wood, and even butchering sides of meat. However, these demanding chores required the girls to work alongside the staff, contributing to their bonding.

The work of the Sisters spanned nearly seventy years, including the difficult times of the two world wars and the Depression. The girls came from all over the State, from a wide range of society. The age range was also wide, 'from small toddlers whose mothers had died or were sickly ... to young women preparing for the Teachers' Certificate examination.'

> It is no wonder there is a sense of family among many who went to St Gertrude's ... while some wrote of the idyllic rural setting of the College, its very distance and isolation was itself the source of much additional pressure and hardship for the girls and the Sisters in later years ... But to dwell on these difficulties would leave much that needs to be acknowledged unsaid. St Gertrude's College was an integral part of the Abbey town and as such was greatly influenced by the life of the Abbey. [90]

The curriculum changed little for forty years; it included the usual range of academic subjects, but also commercial subjects, music, art and crafts. After the 1950s, the isolation was broken down by more frequent trips to the city for sporting, cultural or social events.

In 1965, the last of enrolments were made in primary grades. The Abbot was advised that the Sisters would be withdrawn in the following year unless there were major improvements.

Internal furnishings had to be budgeted by the Monastery. Sister Aloysius Mary McCann, who came to the College in 1966, set about the task of refurbishment. A new school block, completed in 1967, saw the end of the rather austere conditions which had prevailed until then. The Monastery built a new ablution and laundry block; dining and catering areas were upgraded; a new swimming pool was built.

School fees were paid directly to the Monastery; the Sisters kept £5 per paying student for their own needs. By 1970, the Sisters were trying to take control of the College's finances, and did so for six years.

The success of St Gertrude's enabled Bishop Torres to get Community support for the establishment of a boys' college. One of the most profitable farming properties was sold to provide capital. Torres approached the Christian Brothers to provide staff, but they had recently established a school in Perth. The Australian Marist Provincial turned down his request on the grounds of limited resources. Torres went to Europe to see the Superior General of the Marist Order and eventually signed an agreement with the Order just six months before the college was due to open. Under this agreement, the Marists undertook to provide staff for three years, renewable, provided that the Benedictines paid a stipend of £50 ($100) for each Brother and travel and outfitting costs, plus keep, for the original Brothers. New Norcia was to retain control and provide religious services.[91]

Of the four Brothers sent to New Norcia, only one spoke English fluently, Brother Stanislaus Healy. His health was frail but he managed to impress his influence on the College before his untimely death in the fourth year as Headmaster. The Australian Provincial of the Marists provided a New Zealand Brother, Sebastian, and a lay teacher, Roy McKechnie, to start

The balconies and roof line at the rear of St Gertrude's, 1993.

the College. Brother Sebastian was

> a vigorous teacher, disciplinarian, administrator and
> sportsman, a 'man's man', and a spell binding public
> speaker especially on his favourite subject, The Irish
> Question.[92]

St Ildephonsus', the first Marist school in the State, opened
in February 1913, with an enrolment of sixty-three, which was
to almost double by the year's end. It was the beginning of fifty
years of service by the Marist Brothers to education in New
Norcia. The *West Australian* reported on the opening of the
College:

> Bishop Torres and his two colleges are evidently
> guarding jealously the splendid ideals set up for them in
> the dim past. Education along the soundest and best lines
> is one of the Benedictine laws, and it was with this side
> of the work at New Norcia that the visitors were mainly
> impressed.

St Ildephonsus' succeeded despite similar problems to those
faced by its sister college, and rapidly acquired a good
academic reputation, although some agricultural and technical
subjects were also offered, and sport was encouraged. The
academic success was certainly due to the influence of
Brothers Stanislaus and Sebastian.

The problems shared with St Gertrude's were isolation,
unsuitable physical conditions in the buildings, lack of scheme
water and no electricity, the two wars and the Depression, and
the division of control between the teaching staff and the
Abbey. However, there was some benefit in the isolation which
seems

> to have intensified an atmosphere which was every bit as
> exotic as the architecture of the settlement suggests.
> Upwards of three thousand boys passed through New
> Norcia and the two constant and central features of their
> daily experience were the Marist Brothers who taught
> them and the background influence of the Benedictine
> monks.[93]

The daily regime, for the boarders in particular, was almost
monastic. Within the township the two colleges were isolated
from each other, and from the Aboriginal 'orphanages'.
However, deliberate attempts to minimise contact between the
boys and girls could be circumvented.

> All that separated the two schools was the settlement's

cemetery and behind that a paddock in which a few pet emus and wallabies were kept. In the corner of this paddock nearest the girls' college, the nuns had a chicken coop and this quickly developed into a clandestine post office. Girls would volunteer to help 'Sister' take the feed to the hens and while 'Sister' was busy collecting the eggs, the girls would tuck their notes into the overlap between the pinewood palings of the fence.[94]

Under the original agreement between Torres and the Marists, the Benedictines provided virtually everything except staffing and were to retain 'all ordinary pensions and fees.' It was Torres himself who first sought to change this arrangement, finding it irksome. He suggested that the Marists assume full responsibility for the finances and simply hand over any surplus to the Benedictines at the end of the year. The new arrangement operated from the beginning of 1914.

Brother Sebastian left in 1917, but the College continued for some time to maintain its quality. Indeed, the years from 1917 to 1928 were considered to be its 'golden years'.[95] The Depression and World War II followed, no doubt having a major impact, as did social and educational changes in the State in general.

In the Golden Jubilee year of the College, the Marists gave notice that they would withdraw from it. They did so, leaving the College as a solely Benedictine responsibility under the new name of St Benedict's. The Sisters of St Gertrude's and the staff of St Benedict's introduced coeducation in 1973. In the following year the two colleges merged as Salvado College under the leadership of Mr Tony Phelan. By the end of 1976, it was evident that the Sisters could not continue and that 'the dream Torres had for education died with him'.[96] The largesse which marked his involvement with St Gertrude's was not maintained by subsequent Abbots. Although

goodwill was always evident ... the financial and business underpinning of the great venture was seriously lacking. The feudal model of administration evident under Torres could never have carried the great educational adventure into the future.[97]

There is a tragic footnote to the story of the Colleges:

The last Josephite Sister on the staff of Salvado College, Sr Irene McCormack, was assassinated—or one can say martyred—in Peru in 1991 by the Path of the Shining Light guerilla group.[98]

THE BUILDINGS OF NEW NORCIA

R McK Campbell

The buildings of New Norcia were constructed in three periods under the direction of Bishop Salvado (1850–1880s), Bishop Torres (1901–1914), and Father Urbano Gimenez (1915–1930s).

THE SALVADO PERIOD

Once Salvado had chosen the final site, he began to build permanent accommodation for the Mission. A simple stone cottage served as dormitory, refectory, and chapel for the monks. This cottage became the centrepiece of the courtyard around which a U-shaped monastery was built.

Later, the town was laid out on a cruciform plan with the main east-west axis through this cottage. The Church and cemetery were set on this axis with a little brick shrine up the hill at the western end. In 1918 the Apiary was added to stop the eastern end of the line. At a right angle, the north-south axis was the old main road from York to Moora, which runs across the front of the Monastery and on up to the Courthouse.

The early buildings of this period are characterised by the use of natural fieldstones, with mud plaster and limewash, and

The north wing of the Monastery, 1860s. [*Courtesy of Battye Library 74052P*]

Rear view of the Monastery, 1870s. The original cottage in the centre; the north wing at the right; the south wing under construction. [*Courtesy of Battye Library 73636P*]

The Abbey Church, c1870. The timber in the foreground was for use in building the south wing of the Monastery in the 1870s.

[*Courtesy of Battye Library 73539P*]

tree-trunk and bush-pole carpentry and shingle roofs. These materials were gathered around the site and assembled by the monks, with occasional help from Perth or Northam. The buildings remaining from this time are the Flour Mill, the north wing of the Monastery, and the original section of the Church.

The old Flour Mill was built in the 1850s. It is of simple design and plain construction, sufficiently well-built to have survived. After the construction of a new Flour Mill in 1879, the first Mill was used as a practice room for the brass band and later, as a feed store for the adjacent stables.

Close to the old Mill is the original Police Station and Lock-up, now a residence. A stone building with shingle roof (now covered by iron), it has a picturesque quality which belies the original function. South of the old Mill is a cottage of the 1860s, the sole survivor of many built by the monks for Aboriginal couples who settled at the Mission.

The Church, commenced about 1860, has a simple cruciform plan of nave, transepts and sanctuary, of classical proportions but with a rustic feeling because of the rough granite walls and shingle roof. The interior was decorated in a classical theme of Ionic columns and beams painted on the plastered walls. The raised sanctuary was filled with a carved wooden altar, rails and screen. An ornate chandelier hung in the crossing. In the 1870s the sanctuary was extended to form a choir with a decorated pressed metal ceiling, and sacristies were added to the transepts each side.

The north wing of the Monastery was commenced in 1857 to provide for the growing number of monks at New Norcia. It was a two-storey building of fieldstone walls covered by a shingle roof. The intermediate floor was supported on tree-trunk beams. In the 1870s, this wing was extended around the corner to run into the old cottage. This extension contained two floors of bedrooms over a refectory and basement kitchen. This was followed by a matching L-shaped wing south and west back to the road.

In the refectory there are the first signs of some elaboration of detail in the pressed metal ceilings and a carved wooden dado around the walls. On the first floor of the south wing the new chapel was decorated with a hand-made, hand-painted metal ceiling.

In 1874, Garrido Hall, a single-storey wing of workshops, was extended northwards, turning east at the bakery and butcher shop to enclose another courtyard. This wing had solid brick walls, but otherwise the design and details remain the same, and so the new work blended very well with the old. A

Rear view of the Monastery. [*Courtesy of Battye Library 73629P*]

The 'new' Flour Mill, 1993.

brick and iron laundry/workshop, built in the vineyard behind the Monastery, is still in use as a garden shed.

As the Community expanded in the 1870s, accommodation for novices was built across the road from the Monastery; it was later used as a guest house and workers' quarters before being converted finally to the Police Station in the 1950s. It is a simple, two-storey brick house with a corrugated iron roof over the original shingles. The upper level of the double-storey veranda on the east side has been enclosed, but the original woodwork balustrade and valances are intact. A fine sundial (1876) is a feature of the west wall. The building is another good example of the architecture of the Salvado period. It has simple georgian proportions, but the details are of a European tradition which sets it apart from contemporary Western Australian houses. It relates visually to the Monastery and Church and is an essential element in the townscape.

The Cemetery is up the hill from the Church on the east-west axis. As well as being a significant element in the townscape, the graves of monks, nuns, Aborigines and farmers reflect the history of New Norcia. On the path up to the cemetery gates is a statue of Bishop Salvado which was presented by the Spanish Government in the 1960s.

During the expansion and consolidation of the Mission in the 1870s, there were significant changes in construction methods. Brick replaced fieldstones in walls; brickmaking continuing as a lively local industry up to the 1930s. The tree-trunk beams became square-sawn; floor-joists, floor-boards and rafters were sawn to regular sizes; and there are indications that some components were being made off the site.

To cater for a large increase of production, many of the early farm buildings were replaced at this time. A new Flour Mill was commenced in 1879, and was the last building of the Salvado period. It has three stories of solid brick walls, wooden floors and a huge barn roof covered in shingles, still visible inside. It is now electrically powered, but an early boiler and steam engine are still there. The architecture is typical of this period at New Norcia. In spite of a huge interior volume, the exterior has simple proportions, with expressed pilasters and a hipped roof that reduce it to a human scale.

There are still some indications of the 1870s farm in the Blacksmith's Shop and up the hill to the north, in the Shearers' Quarters. In this area, and also still used as residences, are the Courthouse (1876) and the Post and Telegraph Office (1873).

SALVADO THE BUILDER

(Extracts from his diary show that Salvado took a close interest in building work)

1879

1 Sept. I marked the site for the fabrication of the new building of the [flour] mill.

[The machinery for the mill had been ordered from London and through September the diary notes the laying of stones and carting of bricks. Granite fieldstones were laid for the foundations. The clay bricks for the upper walls were handmade.]

31 Oct. They started putting up the bricks on the stone foundations of the new house for the mill.

1880

30 Mar. The carpenters went to cut beams for the new mill.

28 Jun. Brother Domingo left with the spring cart for Newcastle [Toodyay] in order to bring a certain Mr. Charles Morris, the miller of Mr. D. Connor, to get his opinion about the best way to put the beams in the building of our new mill.

30 Jun. ... the miller Charles Morris who seems well informed about the steam mill. We will see the result.

[The machinery arrived in August 1880. Preparations were made to put the first beams into the building in 1881. However setting the main beams in the upper floor proved to be a difficult job.]

1881

30 Mar. This afternoon the two highest beams were put across the room we have reserved for the steam engine of the new mill.

1 Jun. Between Monday and Tuesday and today 8 beams were lifted to the third floor of the new mill besides a lot of the joists for the same floor and thanks be to God all went without incident.

[The beams were tree-trunks, and some have survived.]

28 Jun. This morning the walls of the new building for the mill and granary were finished. It is 80 ft long by 30 ft wide.

[The roof went on in October and, in November, the plastering began. The millstones were set in place in November together with the main axle of the mill and the gearbox.]

1882

14 May. Thanks be to God, the covering of the new mill is completed without incident.

8 Oct. I visited the mill and I remain satisfied with everything. It is completed like no other one in the colony.

The front of the Monastery, 1910. [Courtesy of Battye Library 72817P]

THE TORRES PERIOD

In a period of consolidation around the turn of the century, Bishop Torres made further improvements to the Monastery and Church. The two-storey houses on the road front, immediately north and south of the main buildings, were added to the Monastery in 1901. A third floor was added to the north wing to match the south and, in 1903, the original cottage was finally removed to make way for a new central building with a basement cellar, a hall on the ground floor, and accommodation for the Abbot above. An ornate entrance archway, with wrought iron gates and a screen wall of brick and stucco, was built at this time to close the Cloister across the road front. The ensemble was unified in detail by extending to the new structures the stucco pilaster and window moulding decoration of Salvado's south wing. Wall panels were added to the decorative system and the colour scheme of light wall and dark mouldings was reversed. The statue of St Benedict was added to the cloister in 1932.

In 1908, Torres remodelled the front of the Church and added the campanile in an Italian Renaissance manner. The side walls remained in the Salvado style; corrugated iron roofing was laid over the shingles. Inside, the walls were repainted in a strong Asturian scheme of frieze, pilasters and ceiling decorations. A new ornately carved and gilded altar, rails and screen filled the sanctuary and separated it from the choir.

To cater for an expanding role in community education, Torres set about the construction of a girls' boarding school (opened in 1908). It was named St Gertrude's, and was followed by the boys' equivalent, St Ildephonsus' which opened in 1913. Both buildings are planned in a formal, functional manner with day-rooms on the ground floor and two floors of bedrooms above to accommodate about 150 pupils. They both carried on the theme of red brick with stucco dressings but expressed in quite different architectural styles. There was some involvement of a Spanish architect in the designs, and the end results speak more of southern Europe than of Australia at that time. While both buildings have an unusual and highly decorated Chapel, St Ildephonsus' is generally more restrained in its detail. St Gertrude's shows a wide variety of pressed metal ceiling patterns and painting, an elaborate cast iron veranda, imported European brassware and tiles.

At the rear of St Gertrude's, a tiny cottage was built in the style and detail of the main buildings. A robust brick structure,

The New Norcia Post and Telegraph Office, 1898. The Postmaster, T F Mansbridge in the gateway.
[*Courtesy of Battye Library 73687P*]

The Abbey Church, c1881, before re-modelling by Torres. Note that the wooden belfry has been moved towards the front of the church. [*Courtesy of Battye Library 73521P*]

combining handball courts and an arcaded shelter, was built behind St Ildephonsus'.

The College campus was defined by high red brick walls and rows of eucalypts. The remains of these walls and formal tree plantings, together with carefully placed statues and monuments, contribute to a distinctive townscape quality for the College precinct and the town as a whole.

Following the construction of the Colleges, Torres rebuilt and formalised the existing Mission orphanages to emphasise the educational role for the buildings. St Mary's, in front of St Ildephonsus', and St Joseph's, in front of St Gertrude's, had new classrooms built, and dormitories added on to the old convent accommodation that had developed from Salvado's time.

Building the Apiary, 1918.
[Courtesy of Battye Library 74902P]

St Joseph's Orphanage, built 1909.
[Courtesy of Battye Library 74625P]

The New Norcia Hotel (formerly Hostel), 1993.

FATHER URBANO GIMENEZ

Father Urbano carried on this educational building programme for Abbot Catalan up to the 1930s. A new Convent on the street front became the formal centrepiece of St Joseph's and an important element in the townscape. It is a conscious attempt by Gimenez at a civic statement and pays more attention to formal architectural rules than the work of his predecessors.

At the other end of the street, a two-storey Administration Building, of more restrained proportion and detail, was added to the St Ildephonsus'/St Mary's group. This building is one of the few early red brick buildings in New Norcia left without render or paint. The bold colour and texture of its well-made brickwork make a positive contribution to the townscape.

A Community Guest House, now the New Norcia Hotel, was Fr Urbano's most conspicuous work. It is a monumental and over-scaled building, but again from a classical background with well-ordered and comfortable interior spaces.

At the other end of the architectural scale is the Apiary. This little pavilion is the termination point at the eastern end of the main axis of the town. The timber-framed octagonal building was originally designed and built in 1918 by John Casellas and Rogelio Suarez — Spanish craftsmen employed by the Community. In 1938, its function changed from bee-house to honey factory, and it was extensively remodelled by Fr Urbano.

Other buildings remaining from this period include the Olive Press and Carpenter's Shop built in 1926; the crusher press and boiler are still working. Not still in use is the Piggery. The picturesque cottage will be restored, but the brick and concrete sties are in ruins. Both of these reinforce the picture of the self-sufficient agrarian way of life practised by the Benedictine Community at New Norcia.

Father Urbano Gimenez, 1948.
[Courtesy of Battye Library 73010P]

Rear view of the Monastery, c1940s, Juniorate at the left.
[Courtesy of Battye Library 74102P]

Model of Nervi's design for the new cathedral, 1960.
[Courtesy of Battye Library 74894P]

PIER LUIGI NERVI AND THE DESIGN FOR A NEW CATHEDRAL

John White

New Norcia as we now know it would have been altered drastically if the Benedictine Community had not, in the early 1960s, decided not to proceed with drastic remodelling of the town which would have seen a large new cathedral and monastery built on the slopes of the townsite to the west of the cemetery.

In the late 1950s, the Community, believing it was time for an ambitious rebuilding programme, commissioned the International Institute of Liturgical Arts in Rome to prepare designs for a new cathedral and monastery. The design for the unbuilt Cathedral of the Holy Trinity achieved worldwide acclaim even before the final drawings had been presented to the Community because of its association with the Italian architect/engineer, Pier Luigi Nervi.

In the New Norcia archives there is a series of designs for a new cathedral, by Bishop Torres, Abbot Gusi, Father Urbano Gimenez and Perth architects Henderson and Thompson. None was developed beyond initial design and all followed the pattern of monastic religious architecture which had matured in Europe during the previous millennium. The drawings for the Institute design reveal a progressive modification of design which culminate in a building combining new directions in church planning with dramatic recent technological innovations. The resulting form, symbolising the Trinity to which it was dedicated, had no exact precedent in architecture.

An early drawing shows a conventional layout within a triangular plan shape, but the design developed to take into account new liturgical requirements for church planning then being experimented with. Nervi and his assistants, engaged as consultants by the Institute after the initial stages of design, appear to have increasingly taken over the design. The design which emerged has the unmistakable stamp of Nervi's handling of form and structure as an indivisible whole. The concept drawings and model were published at the time in the international architectural press as Nervi's design.

Abbot Gusi put on paper his suggestion for a new cathedral during a visit to New Norcia in the 1930s and, in 1957, he introduced the Lord Abbot, then in Rome, to members of the International Institute of Liturgical Arts. The Institute was founded in 1955, with the objective of promoting contemporary religious art and architecture.

Nervi established the practice of Nervi and Nebbiosi in

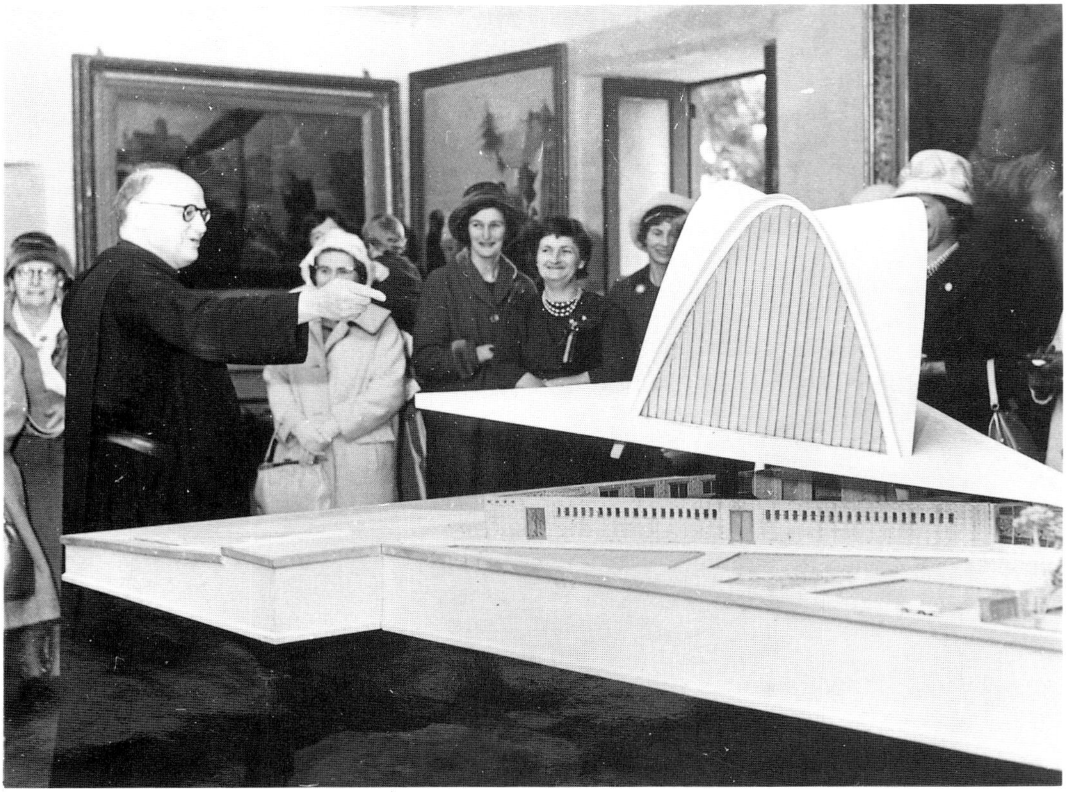

Fr Maur Enjuanes demonstrating the model of Nervi's design for the new cathedral, c1960.
[*Courtesy of Battye Library 74893P*

Model for Nervi's design for the new cathedral, 1960.
[*Courtesy of Battye Library 74896P*]

Rome in 1920; it eventually became Studio Nervi. His important early structures were in Italy but, with a growing reputation, his practice became international. He specialised in the use of reinforced concrete and, in particular, in his own derivation of it which he called 'ferro-cemento'. This was one of the structural techniques adopted for the construction of the proposed cathedral. Its most spectacular characteristic was its soaring triangular vaulted roof supported on three huge parabolic arches enclosing coloured glass walls. Nervi was an architect, engineer and builder, and he sought in his work to bridge the gap between these professions in a way which recalls the mediaeval master-masons whose work he said was truly miraculous.

Nervi and his son, Antonio, were in the team of architects and engineers working on the project. The visual characteristics of the design suggest that there were at least two designers involved in the development of the monastery and cathedral, although they were presented as one project. Nervi's contribution seems to have been restricted to the cathedral. There is some evidence that he was reluctant to accept the commission until he realised the possibilities inherent in designing a cathedral dedicated to the Holy Trinity.

The monastery was designed as a U-shaped building of several storeys enclosing a cloistered garden; a straightforward example of twentieth century functionalism. The design for the cathedral has a quite different character, though its development in detail, from the sublimely beautiful model of the concept published by Nervi in its early stages to the final design, brought it superficially closer to the functionalism of the monastery than Nervi may have wished.

The drawings, correspondence and other materials in the archives reflect the design process: the schedule of requirements drawn up by the Community; the presentation, modification and re-presentation of drawings until final agreement was reached. Although there are some gaps in the drawings in the archives, a considerable number, including rough sketches, and two models showing aspects of the design, survive.

Site drawings show that the proposed buildings were to be placed along an axis running westward from the Abbey Church, through the centre of the Salvado memorial to the vacant land beyond it. The cathedral faced the existing town, rising above it, with the monastery behind to the west. The symbolism is direct and uncomplicated, and the visual character of the design in marked contrast to the character of the then existing buildings of the township; an expression of the present, not a repeat of old visual traditions.

Nervi and the Institute obviously agreed about breaking

from the past to build unashamedly for the present. Nervi saw this as working in the spirit, if not in the image, of the past. At that time, Western Australian architects also, by and large, accepted this view. Conservation, as defined in the 1990s, would not have fitted easily within that climate of architectural opinion. But in Italy (as in other countries damaged by World War II) there was much debate about the wisdom of disregarding the visual characters of towns and their environments to build in new ways which, if insensitively handled, could fracture age-old visual harmonies. We can only judge if this would have been the case in New Norcia by looking at the surviving drawings.

Seen alone, as a building detached from its site and environment, much of the significance of Nervi's design for the cathedral lies in the intrinsic relationship between the floor plan, the structure, the shape of the vaulted canopy above, and the three high stained-glass windows, which together created a symbol for the Trinity.

That expression rested upon symbolic interpretation of the meaning of the Trinity. Number and geometry were important elements of mediaeval religious symbolism. Gothic master-masons evolved an esoteric apparatus of symbols based upon numerical and geometrical relationships which could be used to determine two- and three-dimensional relationships for all parts of a religious building, from the smallest to the largest. The number three, the simplest manifestation of the concept of the Trinity, was not the easiest to represent three-dimensionally when the most complex available structures were based upon circles, squares or rectangles, and greater length was achieved by replication of vaulted bays which, by their nature, were rectangular in plan. Nervi had the means to accomplish what Gothic architects had found impossible. He described Gothic builders as the real forerunners of modern technology, and his description of their art could well be applied to his own:

> The highest expression of Gothic architecture is the large cathedral, and one can only affirm that in these unsurpassed masterpieces of the art of building the fusion of technology and aesthetics is so complete that one cannot separate the constructional aspect from the architectural one.

In his design for the unbuilt Cathedral of the Holy Trinity we can see how he translated the 'fusion of technology and aesthetics' in contemporary terms using the sophisticated twentieth century technology. Distance was his greatest handicap. He never saw the site for his cathedral and whether, if constructed, it would have been the masterpiece suggested by the drawings we shall never know.

MUSIC AT NEW NORCIA

Music has always been an essential element of the Catholic liturgy; it has been an integral part of the life of New Norcia where three major strands of music

> were enmeshed in order to achieve certain social goals in the 19th and early 20th centuries ... the music of the Catholic liturgy, the popular music of Spain and the English speaking world, and middle-class devised Anglo-Australian educational music.[99]

Liturgical music helped to bond the religious community and to reaffirm spiritual values. Salvado knew that music helped to keep the Aborigines contented; the brass band, particularly, made use of the popular music. The third kind of music was

> used as an educational tool to turn out young white Australian farming stock with suitable social aspirations and Aboriginal labourers and domestic servants no longer in receipt of their traditional way of life ... New Norcia used music to promote certain religious and attendant social views among the young.[100]

This was also the practice of other Christian missions in Australia but, at New Norcia 'these three areas of musical endeavour reached a level of both social and aesthetic significance not recorded elsewhere.'[101]

We have already seen that Salvado was a talented musician; he began a strong tradition of music in the life of the Monastery, viewing music 'as a human grace, the gift of God to be employed in His glory, but

> There was nothing of the puritan in his approach allowing, as it did, for dance music and popular songs to find a place in which to sustain everyday mission life.[102]

He attempted to transform Aboriginal chant into European forms. He was

> one of the very few musicians in the country to be in close contact with traditional

Dom Odon Oltra, c1870.
[*Courtesy of Battye Library 73480P*]

125

Aboriginal music and to have an open mind about its significance ... however, very little has yet come to light and that little is in the realm of adaptation, the use of fragments to create a European art work, rather than an attempt to record and analyse.[103]

In the liturgical music, vocal music was emphasised supported by the organ. The organ was also used as a solo instrument. In church and at recreation, stringed music was encouraged. The monks sang Gregorian chant, possibly using forms from Compostela or Cava; the Monastery was one of the few places in Australia, then, where Gregorian chant would have been heard.

One of the band of monks who arrived in 1853 was Dom Oltra.

Much of the reputation of New Norcia as a centre of music was due to his work on the Mission as organist, choir master, music-teacher and band-master ... He began by unifying the monastic choir, training men from varying backgrounds into a single music unit ... This achieved, Oltra began to train the 'native boys' as choristers, at first alternating, then combining with the monks to sing masses and other 2, 3 and 4 part works. The Aboriginal boys were included in order to supply the soprano parts ... [They] learned by rote. From the beginning their prodigious memories astonished everyone who heard them ... Once the choir was formed Oltra turned to teaching the boys to play instruments and for this score reading was needed. He began to teach the boys to read music, then to play whatever instrument they chose from what was available. Within a few months he raised a string orchestra of 20 players and subsequently a brass band of 25.[104]

There is, as yet, not much evidence of the way the Aboriginal girls were involved in music.

Dom Oltra believed that his success with the string orchestra could be repeated with the brass band. When Salvado went to Rome in 1870 he procured a full set of brass instruments.[105] Again Dom Oltra had quick results. The orchestra and the band flourished until the last years of the century. In 1883, Lady Broome, wife of the Governor, visited the Mission and wrote

In front of the wide verandah, on the left, all the school children were drawn up, and, behind them again stood the band. Yes, a regular string band, some eighteen or twenty strong, of native boys; one playing a big double bass, others violins, a 'cello and so forth ...[106]

In 1898, Dom Oltra died of cancer. For some time after his

Brother Odon Oltra playing the organ with a group of pupils, c1870.
[*Courtesy of Battye Library 40453P*]

Monastic musicians, c1910-12. Back row: Frs Urbano, Felix, Veremund, Gullermio, Enrique. Front row: Frs Rosendo, Aloysius, Roberto, Galles, Esteban. [*Courtesy of Battye Library 75381P*]

Frs Eladio Ros and Ramiro Ausejo with St Mary's Orphanage Band, c1945.
[*Courtesy of Battye Library 73038P*]

Father Eladio Ros and some members of the St Mary's Orphanage
Band, c1945. [*Courtesy of Battye Library 73019P*]

death, as there was no Brother to take his place, one of his Aboriginal pupils, Paul Pirimino, took his place as organist and as conductor of the Aboriginal boys' choir and of the string and brass bands.

> In April 1901 ... when Bishop Torres arrived ... Paul was waiting at the gate of the Monastery with a sextet of brass instruments to welcome him and his party of young Benedictines home. He next proceeded with the monks to the church where a solemn *Te Deum* was sung by the monastic choir, Paul sitting at the organ ...[107]

This seems to have been his last public appearance. Efforts by a young monk brought out by Torres to repeat Oltra's success failed and the groups gradually disintegrated.[108] Torres had heard of a young Spanish monk, Dom Stephen Moreno, who showed great promise in his musical training, and arranged special tuition in Rome for him. There, Moreno was influenced by the revival of Gregorian chant in liturgical music. He came to New Norcia in 1908 where, under Torres' patronage, he began a life of composition.[109]

> The long list of Moreno's works includes music for brass band, chamber music, motets, offertories, music for Holy Week, Gregorian chant, masses, Nativity music, orchestral music, music for piano and for organ, secular songs, and other ecclesiastical music ... Vatican II saw the demise of the Latin music tradition. To me this is still a matter of deep regret ... Dom Moreno's music was shelved and left to gather dust as the choir decayed and vocations dwindled ... But the music he has bequeathed is worth reviving.[110]

Dom Moreno, however, seemed to have no interest in training the Aboriginal boys — or lacked Dom Oltra's ability to involve them. In Oltra's day

> the boys were permitted to retain their traditional vocal intonation and no-one thought them any the worse for it, but the new monks introduced by Torres found it offensive. The boys resisted the change over to a European form of intonation.[111]

Moreno believed that the Aborigines 'were incapable of reaching a satisfactory standard in vocal music.' However, Dom Eladio Ros, assistant schoolmaster at St Mary's Orphanage, persisted despite a 'stiff rebuff' from Moreno. In 1937, he began to teach the boys 'more or less behind Moreno's back.' His efforts culminated in a performance of the

Peter Giater (Jater) with a fiddle, 1933.
[*Courtesy of Battye Library 73470P*]

Perosi *Missa Pontificalis.* A reluctant Moreno consented to a hearing and finally gave his blessing and the boys soon became a permanent part of the monastic choir again. Ros became Director of the Orphanage in 1945. With the assistance of Dom Ramirus Ausejo, he revived the boys' brass band, aiming to have it perform during the New Norcia Centenary celebrations in 1946.[112] He was evidently successful.

... the boys furnished a most pleasant surprise by the rapid and effective manner in which they responded to the monks' efforts to train them into a brass band. Their performances in [the choir and band] during the New Norcia celebrations ... were an eye-opener and left no doubt in the audiences as to what these youthful singers and players might achieve.[113]

Moreno was on his way to Spain in 1953 when he developed pneumonia. He was put ashore in Marseilles and admitted to hospital, but died on 5 March. He is buried at the Benedictine Abbey of En-Calcat.

THE PIPE ORGAN IN THE ABBEY CHURCH

Abbot Catalan fulfilled a wish of Torres by sending Dom Moreno to Munich for further studies in composition. During his stay in Europe, Moreno arranged for the purchase of a pipe organ for New Norcia, selecting an instrument built by Albert Moser which had been displayed at the Munich Exhibition. He wrote to Catalan that it was acclaimed as one of the best organs ever built in Germany. The organ arrived at Fremantle in April 1923, where the Port Authority was alarmed at the apparent importation of 'gun-like objects from an erstwhile hostile country' and held it until convinced that it was harmless. In July 1923, Moreno, assisted by his brother Fr Henry Moreno, Fr Boniface Gomez, Bro. Vincent Quindos, and an Aboriginal boy, Harry Weston, began the task of installation. The organ was first played on 15 August, but was not officially opened until 2 September 1923. It is said to have international as well as national importance.

Two views of the Music Room in the Monastery, showing the murals
painted by Father Lesmes, 1993.

The Holy Family — the circle of Francesco Fracanzano. Fracanzano, born in Apulia, Italy, moved to Naples in 1622 to join the studio of Ribera. Here he was influenced by the Venetian School, especially examples of Titian's work seen in Naples. [*Photograph: Victor France*]

THE ART COLLECTION

Although the idea that old buildings are only suitable for museums should be discouraged, it is appropriate that, at New Norcia, one of the buildings, the former Aboriginal Girls' Orphanage, St Joseph's, has been converted to a museum and art galley where some of the rich collections of art and artefacts can be displayed. The Museum and Art Gallery were established by Abbot Bernard Rooney in 1978, acting on the initiative of his predecessor, Abbot Gregory.

Once the Mission was established, Salvado sought books for its library and adornments for the buildings: ornaments, paintings and other art works. When he arrived at New Norcia he brought with him the first painting in the collection, *Our Lady of Good Counsel*. He selected works during trips to Europe; others were collected for him by agents, some ecclesiastical, some lay or commercial. His brother, Father Santos, acted as an agent when he returned to Spain, arranging to dispatch a wide range of things, from flour mill machinery to art works and books. Salvado's successors have continued to add to the collections.

The Art Gallery contains two major collections of paintings: European, principally Italian and Spanish, and modern paintings on religious themes. There are also other art and craft works, ranging from a richly jewelled monstrance to elaborately embroidered vestments.

The European collection may contain few major works, although this cannot be asserted with certainty until the collection has been assessed by experts. Its significance, as Margaret Anderson has written, is that it is a strong collection reflecting the history of the New Norcia Community. Unfortunately most of the European paintings were damaged when thieves cut them from their frames in 1986 and are in storage awaiting restoration.

There is one nineteenth-century English work, a narrative painting by William Cave Thomas, *King Canute Listening to the Monks of Ely*. This work was originally owned by the National Gallery of Victoria. That gallery disposed of some of its large collection of early religious paintings in the

Father Lesmes photographed in his studio in Manila, c1924. [*Courtesy of Battye Library 72680P*]

Brother Salvador and John Casellas, the woodcarvers, c1915.
[*Courtesy of Battye Library 73304P*]

John Casellas and his wife with Mrs Johnston by the buggy and her daughter seated in it, 1915.
[*Courtesy of Battye Library 77994P*]

1940s and New Norcia was able to acquire this painting. The Monks of Ely were Benedictines, famous for their singing.

The Divine Shepherdess, by Juan Fernandez de Laredo (1632-1692), a romantic, pastoral Madonna, was given to Salvado by the Oratorian Fathers, in 1849, when Salvado visited Spain.

Two early watercolours, by an itinerant artist, are a valuable record of the appearance of New Norcia in the 1860s, as well as having much charm as naive works.

Works of the woodcarver John Casellas and the artist Fr Lesmes Lopez, both brought to New Norcia by Bishop Torres to adorn the new and old buildings, are on display in the Gallery. One of Fr Lesmes' largest works is *The Last Supper*, for which the monks of New Norcia were models. Some of their works are not accessible to the public, being in parts of the Monastery. They include the elaborately carved bookshelves of the Library, by Casellas, and the murals on the walls of the Music Room by Fr Lesmes.

Most of the altars at New Norcia were built and carved by Casellas. Two examples of furniture made by him are on display: the Abbot's Throne, and a window seat from the Abbot's site. The latter, unlike much of Casellas' rather baroque carving, is Art Nouveau in style, and must be one of the earlier examples of a major piece in this style produced in Western Australia. It also shows that Casellas, though isolated at New Norcia, was keeping in touch with European art movements.

When so much of the existing collection was damaged by theft, the Monastery set about collecting modern art works on religious themes by distinguished Australian artists, some of whom have generously donated their works. The annual Mandorla Prize for Religious Art gave additional impetus to the development of this collection. Artists represented include: John Coburn, Theo Koning, Joe Furlonger, David Russell, Howard Taylor, Louis Kahan, Alan Baker, Miriam Stannage and Pro Hart. The collection is notable for the rich variety of responses to religious themes.

There are several hundred items in the vestments collection, only a sample being on display, including elaborately hand-embroidered vestments, and those of an Abbot, together with an Abbot's pectoral cross and other jewellery.

The collection of Holy Relics may be the largest in Australia. Among other items on display are three exotic cabinets, of lapis lazuli, ebony and marble; two Spanish painted statues, of wood covered with thin plaster, of St Benedict's sister, St Scholastica, and of St Placid; and an ivory crucifix which was a gift from Queen Isabella of Spain.

In addition, but largely in storage, there is a very large collection of works on paper containing old European engravings, original drawings by community members, botanical watercolours, maps and architectural plans for the New Norcia buildings and interiors, and prints and watercolours depicting the foundation and development of New Norcia itself. Most of the collection dates from the time of the establishment of the community in the mid nineteenth century although there are some works which considerably predate this ... The works on paper are a rich and valuable repository of the history, ideals and values of the Benedictine Community in Western Australia.[114]

The print collection, mostly etchings, engravings and lithographs, include the small lithographs used to illustrate Bishop Salvado's *Memoirs*, and prints from the sixteenth, seventeenth and eighteenth centuries. There is also a large collection of Fr Lesmes' drawings.

THE NEW NORCIA ART GALLERY AND MUSEUM

Margaret Anderson

The art collection at the New Norcia Museum and Art Gallery is perhaps less significant than that at the Abbey Museum (Caboolture, Queensland), but its combination with a strong collection reflecting the history of the Benedictine Community in New Norcia since the 1840s, makes it very significant indeed. In fact New Norcia constitutes a rare resource for the nation: there can be few other sites which combine an original built environment, (consisting of the Abbey itself, two major schools and several groups of houses) with an uninterrupted documentary record of a settlement (including a full run of baptismal, marriage and death records and a valuable photographic archive) and a substantial collection of material culture. The relics collection reflects the material history of New Norcia, from its establishment by Bishop Salvado as a mission to the Aborigines, through its gradual transformation to a general teaching function. In its evidence of the mission's activities it also charts the history of race relations and official racial policy in Australia, in both documentary and material form. The art collection is less clearly documented, but includes the famous *Madonna and Child (Our Lady of Good Counsel)*, brought to Western Australia by Bishop Salvado and popularly believed in the nineteenth century to have saved the original mission from bushfire in the 1840s when the bishop held the painting before the advancing flames.[115]

THE ART THEFT

On 23 January 1986, two men flew from Sydney to Perth, and then travelled to New Norcia by hire car. They entered the Museum and Art Gallery late in the afternoon, waited until other visitors had left, and then locked the door. They bound and gagged the elderly female attendant and then began to remove paintings from their frames.

They worked hastily and roughly, wrenching frames apart and cutting paintings out, attacking half the collection of European religious art. Several valuable seventeenth- and eighteenth-century works were cut but left in their frames, suggesting that the robbers may have become nervous and left before finishing what they had planned. The two men drove back to Perth with the rolled-up paintings in the boot of the car. They hid the paintings overnight in their hotel room and, next day, sent them by truck to Sydney before flying home.

The Perth Major Crime Squad, taking control of the case, traced the hire car and identified the motel where the robbers had stayed. Two senior detectives flew to Sydney and, within two weeks of the robbery, arrested a used-car salesman who confessed to the crime. At his home the detectives found eleven of the paintings and the names of two collaborators. At the home of one of the collaborators they found another eleven paintings. The remaining paintings were found at Sydney airport, wrapped and ready for loading onto an aircraft bound for Manila. All but one of the paintings was recovered; one, *The Annunciation*, had been kicked to pieces because the thieves could not roll it.

Late in 1986, the three men were tried in Perth. It was revealed that an art reproducer was the architect of the crime. He had visited New Norcia the previous year to take photographs of the paintings on display as well as of the Museum's alarm system. The three men involved were convicted and sentenced to serve a minimum of three years. The Benedictine Community subsequently received a written apology from one of them.

Experts have inspected the paintings and have advised that they suffered considerable damage; the cost of restoration being estimated at between $100,000 and $750,000. While the paintings were insured, the cover was inadequate to meet these costs. The Community hopes to raise funds for this work, and for other urgent conservation and restoration work needed at New Norcia.

Virgin and Child (attributed to Murillo); one of the stolen paintings.

Dom Christopher Power, Procurator of the Monastery, and Abbot Bernard Rooney examining
entries for the Mandorla Prize for Religious Art, 1990.

[*Courtesy of West Australian Newspapers*]

New Norcia from the West by an itinerant painter, 1860. [*Photograph: Victor France*]

NEW NORCIA
A.D. 1860

THERE IS A VOICE OF ONE
CRYING IN THE WILDERNESS
PREPARE THE WAY OF THE LORD
Coburn '89

Prepare the Way by John Coburn. This painting was an entry in the Mandorla Prize competition in 1989 and was purchased by the Art Acquistion Fund. Coburn's very large *Curtain of the Sun* hangs in the Sydney Opera House. [*Photograph: Victor France*]

Missionary(Historical Plaque Series), 1984, by Miriam Stannage. One of a series — based on Sesquicentenary historical plaques set in the pavement, St George's Terrace, Perth — exhibited for Western Australia Week in 1987.

[*Photograph: Victor France*]

The Divine Shepherdess by Juan Fernandez de Laredo (1632-1692). The painting depicts the Virgin Mary in the role of Divine Shepherdess. [*Photograph: Victor France*]

THE MUSEUM

The Museum is housed on the ground floor of St Joseph's and has a series of bays along the east wall which are devoted to thematic displays. In the first bay, two large cabinets house Bishop Salvado memorabilia, including his portable compass and sundial and his prayer chart, symbols of both aspects of his character: the practical man of affairs and the religious man. Other items include his coffee maker, a National Bank cheque book (the Community was the bank's first Western Australian client), religious items and personal relics. Personal effects of two other Abbots, Torres and Catalan, are displayed on the opposite side of the Museum.

The next bay has a display of Aboriginal artefacts; a table case nearby has a small display of documents in which the monks, Salvado in particular, recorded considerable detail of the Aborigines and their culture. They are samples of a remarkable archive, one of the best in Australia relating to Aborigines. Some Aboriginal artefacts were sent to Rome and may be seen in the Ethnographic Museum, part of the Vatican Museum.

The monks were always ready to adopt new technologies: photography, agricultural machinery, telegraphy, surveying instruments, etc. The technological display includes the remnants of Fr Santos Salvado's camera (with which many of the photographs in this book were taken), drawing instruments used by Torres to plan buildings, early maps and meteorological records, early telephones and postal equipment, and farming implements. Many of the implements were made by monk blacksmiths. There is an artificial arm, forged by one of them for one of the monks. Some of the telephone and telegraph equipment would have been used by Mrs Cuper who received the telegram announcing Ernest Giles' coming.

Father Emilian Coll, who was presented with a purse of sovereigns by grateful settlers, would have used much of the equipment displayed in two cabinets of medical and pharmaceutical goods and equipment. Again, along with much old-fashioned gear, can be seen evidence of the monks' interest in new technology, including an electric shock machine which was once thought to have therapeutic value.

Amongst the displays of the craft industries, including winemaking, pasta-making, and honey-making are the gold medal for macaroni and the silver medal for olive oil awarded to New Norcia at the 1908 Franco-British Exhibition in London.

Near the display of musical instruments, including the brass instruments used by the Aboriginal boys' band, is a harmonium given to the Drysdale River Mission by Adolf Hitler's German government in recognition of the rescue, by the monks and the Aborigines of the Mission, of two German aviators, Bertram and Klausman. The harmonium was damaged in a Japanese air raid during World War II.

A green painted long-case clock, against the west wall, was another of Queen Isabella's gifts to the Community.

This very eclectic museum collection epitomises the rich variety of the history and the life of the New Norcia Community.

Agricultural implements in the New Norcia Museum, most of them made by monk blacksmiths.

THE STAMP COLLECTION

Father Kevin Long

While New Norcia's art and book collections are well known and appreciated by both the general public and antiquarians, the Monastery's stamp collection remains an unexplored treasure trove. Until recently, most of the collection was hidden away in disused chocolate and lolly tins, which are themselves museum pieces. The early monks patiently sorted thousands of stamps into neat bundles, tied with an assortment of richly-coloured cotton threads. The assembled stamps reflect the strong European and colonial connections of the community. Spanish, Italian, Vatican and pre- and post-Federation Australian stamps are the numerically stronger sections. Postal stationery, postmarks, envelopes and collectors' catalogues dating back to the last century add a further unique and unifying element. Described more accurately as an *accumulation*, rather than as a *collection*, these philatelic treasures await scholarly classification and professional care; they are a significant part of the monastic heritage.

THE LIBRARY AND ARCHIVES AT NEW NORCIA

Monks are required by the Rule of St Benedict to study; a library, then, is indispensable for a Benedictine monastery. In the isolation of nineteenth-century New Norcia, it is probable that a monastery could not have survived without one. The growth of the book collection at New Norcia can be seen in the more general context of other monastic collections:

> The growth of a monastic collection of books in the Middle Ages was always haphazard. There was rarely any attempt to 'create' or to 'develop' or to 'bring up to date' a library, save in the fifty years after the Conquest, when the abbot of a newly founded or reorganised house might collect books and make arrangements for their multiplication, as was done by a succession of abbots of St Albans. After the twelfth century the growth of a library depended almost wholly upon chance; the tastes or needs of an abbot or individual monk; the demands of teachers or scholars when the monks began to frequent universities; bequests of all kinds; the changing devotional practices of the community. Extant catalogues suggest that by far the most valuable accessions came at the death of a superior or of a monk of distinction or at least of individuality who had supplemented the general store with a small collection of specialised books, as it might be theology or canon law, Latin classical authors, medical books, French poetry, alchemy and astrology, English devotional literature. Consequently, the monastic library, even the greatest, had something of the appearance of a heap even though the nucleus was an ordered whole; at the best it was a sum of many collections, great and small, rather than a planned, articulated unit.[116]

Whereas books played little part in the lives of the Swan River colonists, things were different at New Norcia, where the establishment of a library and the privileging of the act of reading can be seen as consequences of the *Rule of St Benedict* that shapes, informs and gives both coherence and a sense of ultimate purpose to all aspects of the lives of the monks.[117]

On the 6 February 1874, Salvado wrote to Dom Berengier at Solesmes in France:

> My intention is to establish, little by little, a library in this desert of Australia, as large as possible. A monastic

community without books is like an army without arms ...
But in truth, our position, obliged to clear the bush and
make our own bread, to raise sheep, cows and horses for
what they can provide for us, and to make bricks and
timber frames so that we will not have to sleep in the open
air, as we did at first, is it not ridiculous that we claim to
be busy with polyglots and patrologies? Ridiculous or not
it is the truth; and, instead of regretting it, I am determined to add as much as I can to our small library; for
man does not live by bread alone ... What library may we
turn to, in the depths of the bush? Doubtless you will say
that since we live among savages it would not seem likely
that we have grave matters to examine and perplexing
cases to solve. However, only recently, if we had not a
copy of St Thomas' *Summa* to hand, we would not have
known how to resolve a difficulty relating to the baptism
of an adult ... But I'm wrong to feel I must prove to you
the need for a library ... you are a Benedictine monk ...[118]

Salvado began collecting books before the library had been
built; he gathered them — as he had gathered art works and
ornaments — on his trips to Europe. Some books were donated
by the Papacy, others by Queen Isabella, probably at the insti-
gation of Fr Santos Salvado, her confessor. Monastic libraries
in Spain, Italy and England, as well as the Congregation of
Propaganda Fide, also contributed books. Salvado's successors
continued to build up the library, their selections reflecting
both their own particular interests as well as the development
of the publishing industry, particularly the more recent publishing industry of Australia and Western Australia in particular.[119]

As, at first, there was no library for safe housing of the
books there is

a history of accidental dispersal and occasional loss ... that
has persisted almost to the present day, exacerbated by the
destruction by fire of books housed away from the
monastery and by the loss of ships' cargoes during times
of war.[120]

It is inevitable that a collection acquired in this way should
be richly eclectic, bordering on the haphazard, which, it appears
is a characteristic of most monastic libraries. It has been said of
the New Norcia library, before reorganisation began in 1991,
that you could often not find the book you were looking for, but
you would usually be surprised by what you could find.

The collection contains many valuable early imprints; cata-
loguing of these has only recently been completed. The oldest
work, published in 1508, is a copy of the *Margarita*

Philosophica, a treatise on the sciences and the arts of the time: grammar, mathematics, astronomy and medicine.[121] The collection includes approximately 2500 pre-1801 volumes, comprising almost 1300 individual titles. It is one of the best collections of its kind in Australia and contains a number of items which appear to be unique.[122] There is also a comprehensive collection of 'classics' — 'works of profane literature composed before 200AD' — and books on architecture, and 'an impressive collection of Australiana'.[123]

> Small by comparison with many European collections, the New Norcia library is nonetheless significant both for its coherence and for the insights it affords into the development of a religious community which gave books a central place in the lives of the monks ...[124]

There are, as would be expected, a number of copies of the *Rule of St Benedict* — forty-four of the copies printed before 1801, the oldest dating from 1602 — and twenty-six editions of commentary on interpretations of the *Rule*, and also valuable editions of historical works by Benedictine scholars, including works of criticism and defence of monasticism at various times. The collection can be compared with the contents of other monastic libraries, particularly other Benedictine ones.

> ... much of what it contains one might equally have expected to discover in the Benedictine monasteries of Madrid, Solesmes, Downside, or St Martin. Indeed it is certain that even where provenance details do not explicitly confirm it, many of the works at New Norcia once belonged to these ancient Benedictine houses. It is nevertheless undeniable that the library has a recognisably individual as well as traditional character. Salvado's own preferences can be identified as a modest sub-category, though it is significant that most of his choices could also be subsumed under the criterion of general usefulness.[125]

The Library in the Monastery is not open to the general public. However, beginning in 1993, a substantial part of the book stock has been progressively transferred to the New Norcia Library, housed in the library building and attached biology laboratory of the former Salvado College. It is in the grounds of the former St Ildephonsus' College. Some books from the library of Salvado College have been incorporated. The total number of books in the New Norcia collection is believed to be between 70,000 and 80,000.

> The plan is to re-site approximately 60,000 books to the new building; some 25,000 secular titles which have

already been moved there, and over 30,000 religious titles. Split into two definite sections, the library will offer facilities such as research rooms and database searching for both male and female academics, something that has not previously been possible ... About 12,000 volumes will be retained in the monastery, mainly in the rare book room and the new reading room.[126]

It is hoped that the bulk of the stock will be both catalogued and rehoused by the year 2002.

The New Norcia Library is already one of Western Australia's largest libraries outside the Perth metropolitan area. Once the valuable raw materials are transformed into a professionally functioning library it will be a true centre of excellence.[127]

THE ARCHIVES

As with the books, so with the archives; for many years the large and valuable collections were inadequately housed, largely unorganised and uncatalogued, although New Norcia has always had historian monks who knew the value of keeping records. With the appointment of an archivist, considerable progress has been made and the Archives will be more readily accessible to scholars. In 1991, the Community established an Archives, Research and Publications Committee which, as part of its brief, would prepare and oversee programmes of work for the Archives. This book is an early initiative of the Committee.

The bookshelves in the Monastery Library were made by John Casellas, c1910. [*Courtesy of Battye Library 72813P*]

One of the most urgent programmes is the translation of the large part of the Archives which is written in Spanish or, occasionally, Italian or Latin. Some of the monks and Abbots kept diaries. This rich resource will not be fully accessible until translation is completed.

There are voluminous collections of correspondence, farm management records, parish and mission registers, college and orphanage administration records, maps and photographs.

In the early 1980s, the State Archives accessioned and microfilmed the diaries of Salvado, Garrido and Torres, and much of the nineteenth and early twentieth century material organised by Dom Eugene Perez. Access to some of this microfilm is possible only on application to the Superior of the Benedictine Community. The microfilms include some one thousand maps, many hand-drawn by Salvado on tissue and now too fragile to handle.

Of particular value are records of the Noongar people. Among the earliest and most important sources for the elucidation of medieval European demography is the 'Polyptique' or estate inventory drawn up by order of Irmion, abbot from 806 to 829 of the Benedictine house of St Germain-des-Pres in the Ile de France. Just as this provides a baseline for investigating European population estimates and structures from the early ninth century onward, so another Benedictine abbey, that of New Norcia in Western Australia, drew up in 1858 lists of 740 named Aborigines, which must be among the most valuable sources available for studying nineteenth-century Aboriginal populations in Australia.[128]

Fr Eugene Perez, Fr Ramiro Ausejo (at rear), and Abbot Gregory Gomez (foreground) in the Library, c1946.
[*Courtesy of Battye Library 73107P*]

CONTRIBUTORS

Father David Barry, OSB is the Sub-Prior and Novice Master at New Norcia.

Robin McK Campbell is a leading conservation architect in Western Australia.

Faye Davis is a writer of fiction and poetry.

Ben Drayton is an Educational Liaison Officer with the Education Department in Moora.

Elizabeth Jolley is one of Australia's best-known writers.

Father Kevin Long is a Lecturer at the University of Notre Dame.

Wendy Pearce is the Archivist at New Norcia.

Dom Christopher Power, OSB is Procurator of New Norcia.

Abbot Bernard Rooney, OSB is a former Abbot of New Norcia.

Father Placid Spearritt, OSB is the Prior-Administrator of New Norcia.

Tom Stannage is Associate Professor of History at the University of Western Australia.

Trevor Walley is a Wild Life Officer with the Department of Conservation and Land Management.

John White is a former Lecturer in Architecture at the University of Western Australia.

ILLUSTRATION CREDITS

Most of the illustrations are from the rich photographic archive of New Norcia, housed at the Battye Library. We are grateful to the *West Australian* for permission to reproduce photographs from their collection. Victor France photographed the paintings from the Art Collection. Other photographs were taken by David Hutchison.

NOTES

1. Patrick Leigh-Fermor, *A Time to Keep Silence*, Penguin Books, London, 1988. p. 7.
2. R W Southern, *Western Society and the Church in the Middle Ages*, Penguin Books, London, 1986, p. 217.
3. Timothy Fry OSB, (ed) *The Rule of St Benedict in English*, The Liturgical Press, Collegeville, Minnesota, 1981.
4. Southern, pp. 222-223.
5. Leigh-Fermor, p. 35.
6. Fr Placid Spearritt OSB, 'The traditional monastery as a means of communicating the Faith', in *The Australian Catholic Record*, lxxi, 1994.
7. Fry, p. 95
8. Bro Valerian Braniff FMS, St Ildephonsus' College, New Norcia. 1913-1964: An Educational, Religious and Social History, M. Phil. thesis, Murdoch University, Western Australia, 1984, p. 10.
9. ibid.
10. Fry, pp. 11-13.
11. ibid., pp. 21-25.
12. ibid., pp. 69-70.
13. ibid., pp. 75-77.
14. ibid., pp. 61-62.
15. ibid., pp. 62-63.
16. Sylvia Hallam, 'Bishop Salvado and "The Australians"', *New Norcia Studies,* No. 1, April 1993, pp. 31-44.
17. New Norcia Archives 00538
18. Leandre Fonteinne, 'Letters of Leandre Fonteinne, Novice of the Abbey of Solesmes and member of the Western Australian Mission Band 1845-47', trans. Dom Louis Soltner, Dom David Barry, Father Martinus Crawley, Sister Marie Gregory Forster, in *Tjuringa*, Nos 17-25, 1979-83.
19. Fonteinne, p. 84.
20. In some references spelt Tootel or Tuttle.
21. Fonteinne, p. 96.
22. Bishop Rosendo Salvado OSB, *Salvado Memoirs: Historical Memoirs of Australia and particularly of the Benedictine Mission of New Norcia and of the habits and customs of the Australian natives,* trans. E.J. Stormon SJ, University of Western Australia Press, Nedlands, 1977, p. 35.
23. ibid., p. 39.
24. Hallam, p. 31.
25. Salvado, p. 45.
26. ibid., p. 53.
27. ibid., p. 49.
28. ibid.
29. ibid.
30. ibid.
31. Salvado, p. 54.
32. Fonteinne, p. 99.
33. ibid., p. 100.
34. ibid., p. 56.
35. ibid., p. 60.
36. ibid., pp. 66-67.
37. G Russo, *Lord Abbot of the Wilderness — The Life and Times of Bishop Salvado*, Polding Press, Melbourne, 1980, p. 56.
38. D F Bourke, *The History of the Catholic Church in Western Australia*, Archdiocese of Perth, 1978, p. 111.
39. Russo, Pt 1, Chap. 8.
40. Fonteinne, p. 90.
41. J T Reilly, *Reminiscences of Fifty Years Residence in Western Australia,* Sands & McDougall, Perth, 1903, p. 15.
42. Judith M Woodward, 'Manuel Beleda, 1853-1885: his association with the Mission at New Norcia', *New Norcia Studies*, No. 2, June 1994, p. 31.
43. ibid., p. 26.
44. ibid., p. 32.
45. ibid., p. 32.
46. ibid., p. 29.
47. See Bourke, p. 111 et seq., and Russo, Pt 1, Chaps 11-13.
48. Bourke, p. 113.
49. Russo, Pt 2, Chap. 7.
50. ibid., Pt 2, Chap. 9.
51. *Inquirer*, 27 Feb. 1848.
52. Tilbrook, Lois, *Nyungar Tradition: Glimpses of Aborigines of South-West Australia 1829-1914*, University of Western Australia Press, Nedlands, 1983 p. 47.
53. Salvado, pp. 37-38.
54. Hallam, pp. 31-44.
55. ibid.
56. Salvado, p. 69.
57. ibid., p. 78.
58. 'DBL', 'A century of achievement', *St Ildephonsus' College Magazine 1946*, New Norcia, 1947.
59. ibid., p. 73.
60. Quoted in Father James Flood, *New Norcia: the remarkable Aboriginal Institution of the Australian Commonwealth situated in the State of Western Australia: A Monument of Benedictine Courage, Patience, and Charity. A Tribute of an Irish Secular Priest*, Burns and Oates, London, 1908.
61. Neville Green & Lois Tilbrook, *Aborigines of New Norcia: 1854-1904,* (Vol. VII of *The Bicentenary Dictionary of Western Australians*),

University of Western Australia Press, Nedlands, 1989.

62. 'DBL', p. 50.

63. Green & Tilbrook, p. xvii.

64. Tilbrook, op. cit., 47.

65. W E Roth, 'Royal Commission on the Condition of the Natives', (Paper No. 5, *Votes and Proceedings of Parliament, Second Session, 1905*) Perth, Government Printer, 1905.

66. ibid., pp. 118-120.

67. ibid.

68. Green & Tilbrook, p. xix.

69. ibid.

70. Braniff, p. 11.

71. Willaway, Gabby, 'Gabby Willaway' in Colin Glass & Archie Weller (eds), *Us Fellas: An Anthology of Aboriginal Writing,* Artlook Books, Perth, 1987, p. 155.

72. Flood, p. 109.

73. Willaway, pp. 156-157.

74. Susan Maushart, *Sort of a Place Like Home: Remembering the Moore River Native Settlement,* Fremantle Arts Centre Press, 1993, p. 195.

75. Bishop Fulgentius Torres OSB, *The Torres Diaries 1901-1914,* trans. Dom Eugene Perez OSB, Artlook, Perth, 1987.

76. Braniff, pp. 18-19.

77. New Norcia Archives, 00546.

78. Abbot Bernard Rooney OSB, 'Nyungar,Windjar Kurl? (Nyungar, where are you going?): A personal perspective', *New Norcia Studies,* No. 2, June 1994, pp. 11- 18 is a fuller version of this paper.

79. MS. Community diary written by Salvado, translated by Fr Eugen Perez.

80. ibid.

81. ibid.

82. Giles' quotations from Ernest Giles, *Australia Twice Traversed: the Romance of Exploration/ being a narrative compiled from the journals of five Exploring Expeditions into and through Central South Australia and Western Australia from 1872 to 1876,* Sampson, Low, Marston, Searle and Rivington, London, 1889.

83. A shortened version of Tom Stannage, 'New Norcia in History', *New Norcia Studies,* No. 1, April 1993, pp. 1-8.

84. Braniff, p. 19.

85. ibid., pp. 3-4.

86. ibid., p. 4.

87. Sister Leonie Mayne RSJ, 'The Sisters of St Joseph; their contribution to Catholic education in New Norcia', *New Norcia Studies,* No. 2, June 1994, p. 50.

88. Braniff, p. 21.

89. Anon., in Dom Francis Byrne OSB, *80th Anniversary: St Gertrude's College New Norcia, 1908-1988,* New Norcia, 1988, p.9. (There is evidence that the quotation was written by Sr Fintan)

90. Mayne, p. 153.

91. Braniff, pp. 21-22.

92. ibid., p. 23.

93. ibid., p. 8.

94. ibid., p. 53.

95. ibid., p. 71.

96. Mayne, p. 57.

97. ibid.

98. ibid., p. 48, fn.

99. Therese Radic, 'The Music of New Norcia', *New Norcia Studies,* No. 1, April 1994, p. 9.

100. ibid.

101. ibid.

102. ibid., p. 11.

103. ibid.

104. ibid., p. 12.

105. 'DBL', p. 52.

106. ibid., p. 51.

107. ibid., p. 52.

108. Radic, p. 15.

109. ibid., p. 17.

110. ibid., p. 19.

111. ibid., pp. 16–17.

112. ibid.

113. 'DBL', p. 51.

114. Janda Gooding, 'The New Norcia Collection of Art-works on Paper', *New Norcia Studies,* No. 1, April 1993, pp. 21–26.

115. Margaret Anderson, *Heritage Collections in Australia, Report of the Heritage Collections Working Group,* National Centre for Australian Studies, 1991, p. 55.

116. Dom David Knowles, *The Religious Orders of England, Vol II: The End of the Middle Ages,* Cambridge University Press, 1955, p. 332.

117. John Hay, & David Bean, *The early imprints of New Norcia,* Western Australian Institute of Technology, Perth, 1986.

118. Quoted, ibid., p. 4.

119. ibid., pp. 4–5.

120. ibid., p. 4.

121. Trevis C Lawton, 'History among the trees; the New Norcia Library', *Australian Library Journal,* November, 1993, p. 253.

122. *Amici Bibliothecae,* Vol. 3, No. 1, New Norcia, March 1994, p. 3.

123. Hay & Bean, p. 16.

124. ibid., p. 19.

125. ibid., p. 17.

126. Lawton, p. 253.

127. ibid., p. 254.

128. S J Hallam, 'Aboriginal demography in Southwestern Australia: Census Lists', in Green & Tilbrook (eds).

BIBLIOGRAPHY

Anderson, Margaret. *Heritage Collections in Australia, Report of the Heritage Collections Working Group.* National Centre for Australian Studies, 1991.

Benedictine Community of New Norcia. *The Story of New Norcia: the Western Australian Benedictine Mission.* New Norcia, 1991.

Bourke, D F. *The History of the Catholic Church in Western Australia.* Archdiocese of Perth, 1978.

Braniff, Br Valerian, FMS. St Ildephonsus' College, New Norcia 1913–64: An Educational, Religious and Social History. M. Phil. thesis, Murdoch University, Western Australia, 1984.

Byrne, Dom Francis, OSB. *80th Anniversary: St Gertrude's College New Norcia, 1908–1988.* New Norcia, 1988.

'DBL'. 'A century of achievement', *St Ildephonsus' College Magazine 1946.* New Norcia, 1947.

Drayton, Ben. 'The Mission: a first-hand experience'. *New Norcia Studies,* No. 1, April 1993, pp. 27–30.

Flood, Fr James. *New Norcia: the remarkable Aboriginal Institution of the Australian Commonwealth situated in the State of Western Australia: A Monument of Benedictine Courage, Patience, and Charity. A Tribute of an Irish Secular Priest.* Burns and Oates, London, 1908.

Fonteinne, Leandre. *Letters of Leandre Fonteinne, Novice of the Abbey of Solesmes and member of the Western Australian Mission Band 1845–47.* Trans. Dom Louis Soltner, Dom David Barry, Father Martinus Crawley, Sister Marie Gregory Forster. *Tjuringa,* Nos 17–25, 1979–1983.

Garrido, Father V, OSB. 'The Reverend V. Garrido to the Honourable the Colonial Secretary, 8–19'. *Information Regarding the Habits and Customs of the Aboriginal Inhabitants of Western Australia compiled from various sources, 1871.* Legislative Council of Western Australia.

Giles, Ernest. *Australia Twice Traversed: the Romance of Exploration/ being a narrative compiled from the journals of five Exploring Expeditions into and through Central South Australia and Western Australia from 1872 to 1876.* Sampson Low, Marston, Searle & Rivington, London, 1889.

Giminez, Dom William, OSB. 'Twenty-five years in retrospect: St Ildephonsus' College: 1913–38'. *St Ildephonsus' College Magazine 1938.* New Norcia, 1938.

Gooding, Janda, 'The New Norcia Collection of Artworks on paper'. *New Norcia Studies,* No. 1, April 1993, pp. 21–26.

Green, Neville & Tilbrook, Lois. *Aborigines of New Norcia: 1845–1914 (*Vol VII of *The Bicentenary Dictionary of Western Australians.* University of Western Australia Press, Nedlands, 1989.

Haebich, A. *For Their Own Good: Aborigines and Government in the South West of Western Australia, 1900-1940.* University of Western Australia Press, Nedlands, 1988.

Hallam, Sylvia, 'Bishop Salvado and "The Australians"'. *New Norcia Studies,* No 1, April 1993, pp. 31–44.

Hay, John & Bean, David. *The Early Imprints at New Norcia: A bibliographical study of pre-1801 books in the Benedictine Monastery Library at New Norcia, Western Australia.* (Western Library Studies 9.) The Library, Western Australian Institute of Technology, Perth, 1986.

Lawton, Trevis C. 'History among the trees: the New Norcia Library'. *The Australian Library Journal,* November 1993, pp. 250–254.

McMahon, John T. *Bishop Salvado (Founder of New Norcia).* Abbey Press, New Norcia, 1943.

Maushart, Susan, *Sort of a Place Like Home: Remembering the Moore River Native Settlement.* Fremantle Arts Centre Press, 1993.

Mayne, Sr Leonie, RSJ. 'The work of the Sisters of St Joseph and their contribution to Catholic education in New Norcia', *New Norcia Studies,* No. 2, June 1994, pp. 47–58.

Perez, Fr E F, OSB ('Monachus'). *New Norcia 1846–1946: Historical Guide to all its Institutions.* The Benedictine Abbey, New Norcia, 1946.

Perez, Fr E F, OSB. 'Dom Salvado's New Norcia: an account of his mission in Western Australia, 1846–1900'. Bound typescript, Benedictine Archives, New Norcia.

Radic, Therese. 'The Music of New Norcia', *New Norcia Studies,* No 1, April 1993, pp. 9–20.

Reilly, J T. *Reminiscences of Fifty Years Residence in Western Australia.* Sands & McDougall, Perth, 1903.

Revell, Geoffrey, 'Dom Moreno and the New Norcia Organ'. *New Norcia Studies,* No. 2, June 1994, pp. 75–78.

Rooney, Abbot Bernard, OSB. 'Nyungar, windjar kurl?: Cultural awareness — a challenge for the 90s'. *New Norcia Studies,* No. 2, June 1994, pp. 11–18.

Roth, W E. *Royal Commission on the Condition of the Natives (Paper No. 5, Votes and Proceedings* of Parliament, Second Session, 1905). Perth, Government Printer, 1905.

Russo, G. *Lord Abbot of the Wilderness — The Life and Times of Bishop Salvado*. Polding Press, Melbourne, 1980.

Salvado, Bishop Rosendo, OSB. *Salvado Memoirs: Historical Memoirs of Australia and particularly of the Benedictine Mission of New Norcia and of the habits and customs of the Australian Natives*. Trans. E J Stormon SJ. University of Western Australian Press, Nedlands, 1977.

Spearritt, Fr Placid, OSB. 'The traditional monastery as a means of communicating the Faith'. *The Australian Catholic Record*, lxxi, 1, January 1994, pp. 22–22.

Stannage, Tom. 'New Norcia in history'. *New Norcia Studies*, No. 1, April 1993, 1–8.

Tilbrook, Lois. *Nyungar Tradition: Glimpses of Aborigines of South-West Australia 1829–1914*. University of Western Australia Press, Nedlands, 1983.

Torres, Bishop Fulgentius, OSB. *The Torres Diaries 1901–1914*. Trans. Dom Eugene Perez OSB. Artlook Books, Perth, 1987.

Willaway, Gabby. 'Gabby Willaway', in Glass, Colin & Weller, Archie (eds), *Us Fellas: An Anthology of Aboriginal Writing*. Artlook Books, Perth, 1987.

Woodward, Judith M. 'Manuel Beleda, 1853–1885, and his association with the Mission at New Norcia'. *New Norcia Studies* No. 2, June 1994, pp. 21–36.